V-Twin

THE CLASSIC MOTORCYCLE
1903 TO THE PRESENT

Roger W. Hicks

BLANDFORD PRESS
POOLE · DORSET

First published in the UK 1985 by Blandford Press,
Link House, West Street, Poole, Dorset, BH15 1LL

Distributed in the United States by
Sterling Publishing Co., Inc.,
2 Park Avenue, New York, N. Y. 10016.

British Library Cataloguing in Publication Data

Hicks, Roger W.
    V-Twin : the classic motorcycle.
    1. Vincent, H.R.D. motorcycle—History
    I. Title
    629.2'275   TL448.V53

ISBN 0 7137 15022

Typeset by Graphicraft Typesetters Limited
Printed in Spain by Graphicromo S.A.

Contents

Preface

Anyone who tries to define the word 'classic' is on dangerous ground, for one man's classic is another man's dog and – among motorcyclists especially – there are always those for whom anything new is better than anything old, or for whom anything old is better than anything new.

The sense in which I have used 'classic' here is slightly different from the way that it is normally used. Rather than concentrating on individual classic motorcycles, I have concentrated on a classic design, the V-twin. Some of the motorcycles in here are classics by any definition, while others most certainly are not, but the V-twin design, which was comparatively rare when I started the book, has suddenly returned to popularity with a vengeance. Since I began my research, all four of the major Japanese companies have introduced new V-twins, often bearing out what I had predicted! While this is gratifying in one way, because we all like to be proved right, it means that the latest offerings can not be covered in the detail I would wish. Nevertheless, I hope that this book will still prove interesting and thought-provoking.

This is not, and does not attempt to be, a competitor for the many one-marque histories which are available. Instead, it aims to show the different marques and the V-twin in general in context. The text is as accurate as it is possible to make it but, of necessity, not all of the motorcycles illustrated are strictly 'kosher'. Purists will spot an A10 regulator box on a certain Brough Superior, and the brass saddle rivets on one of the Vincents may make some people throw up their hands in horror. I may even have a date slightly wrong on one, maybe two of the machines: even the owners are not infallible, though most are extraordinarily knowledgeable about their machines, so any mistakes are likely to be mine. If there is an error which you feel strongly about, then the publisher will forward your letters to me (provided that you are not actually abusive!); I shall be grateful and – with any luck – the mistake will be corrected in a second edition.

I hope that even buffs of motorcycle history will learn something from this book – after all, how often do you see a picture of a Beaumont Radial? – and that it will prove a useful introduction for newcomers to the fascinating world of classic bikes.

R. W. H.
Bristol 1985

Acknowledgements

It is impossible to produce a book of this kind without help from many people, and I should like to express my gratitude to everyone who so kindly made machines available for photography, particularly the following.

Three Cross Motorcycles, Woolsbridge Industrial Estate, Three Legged Cross, Wimborne, Dorset, who maintain one of the most impressive showrooms full of 'superbikes' in England, and to whom I am indebted for pictures of modern Harley-Davidsons, Ducatis and Moto-Guzzis.

Bill Little Motorcycles of Mandeville, Oaksey Road, Upper Minety, Malmesbury, Wiltshire. Bill's stock is immense and fascinating, and I am very grateful for the way in which he allowed me not just to photograph the bikes, but also to handle them and position them just as I wanted. Machines from his stock in these pages include AJS, Brough Superior, BSA and Indian.

Many other people supplied individual machines, or sometimes two or three. I would particularly like to thank three Bristol firms. Bob Saunders of 1 Belmont Street, Easton, arranged for me to photograph a beautifully restored Indian as well as a superb tartan-tank Douglas on page 72; Bristol Classic Bikes of 17 Church Road, Redfield, provided a Brough Superior as well as a Vincent; and Bob George of APS Motorcycles loaned his own 1946 flathead. Among private individuals, I am grateful to Norton McCombe, whose AJS outfit appears in Chapter 1 and whose Morgan adorns Chapter 6; to Ken Sprayson, who rode his amazingly long Ariel-MAG (page 55) to a spot convenient for photography; to Mr Daw, of Cheltenham, who rode his James to two or three locations for the same purpose; to David Barker of Bath, who not only allowed me to photograph his Tri-King, but even let me drive it; and to all the gentlemen whom I met at the VMCC Founders' Day Rally 1984, some of whose names I have regrettably mislaid, but who include Douglas Atkinson-Losh (Ducati 750 Desmo) and Fred Slaughter (680 Brough).

Among manufacturers and importers, Moto-Guzzi's publicity department in Mandello del Lario was magnificently helpful, and their British importers Coburn and Hughes were also very kind; Harglo Ltd of Solihull, the Moto Morini importers, furnished invaluable information and pictures; BMW (GB) Ltd deserve thanks for help not only with this book, but with others in the past; while the British arms of both Honda and Yamaha kindly supplied many pictures and a good deal of technical information; Babs Ryan of Kawasaki telexed Japan for a picture of the Vulcan, after the book had been completed (and revised!); and Mick Broom of Hesleydon Ltd (Hesketh) devoted the better part of a day to my inquiries and taught me a great deal not only about Heskeths, but also about motorcycle design generally.

The East Midlands Allied Press kindly gave me the run of their extensive archives, and much of the vintage artwork as well as about fifteen of the motorcycles on these pages are from that source. I should particularly like to thank Peter Maskell.

Finally, I should like to thank the National Motorcycle Museum, Coventry Roads, Bickenhill, Solihull, West Midlands for help, for encouragement and for just existing, as well as for several of the detail shots of V-twin engines. It is a treasure-house of British motorcycles of all kinds, and I heartily commend it as a place of pilgrimage for any motorcyclist or motorcycle enthusiast.

1
The Lure of the Vee

In the long and tangled history of motorcycling all sorts of engine layouts have been tried, ranging from the elegant and simple single-cylinder to the absurdly complicated 5-cylinder radial of the 1921 Megola, the water-cooled V8 Moto-Guzzi racer of 1955, and the double overhead cam straight six, pioneered in road bikes by Benelli in 1975 with the Sei 750.

There has, however, always been one layout traditionally used for powerful engines, which is definitely a classic: the V-twin. Ask any motorcycle addict to name the six bikes he would most like to own, from any period in history, and it will be a miracle if there is not at least one V-twin among them.

Names which immediately spring to mind are Harley-Davidson, Brough Superior, Vincent, Ducati and Hesketh, and a little thought brings forth

Ducati 600 TL, 1982.

Opposite:
AJS 1000cc, 1927.

Right: Brough Superior
SS80, 1936.

Opposite:
James 750cc, 1923.

many more: Indian, McEvoy-Anzani, Crocker, Moto-Guzzi, Moto Morini, Matchless, Excelsior ... some of these names will only be familiar to a few V-twin devotees, while others will be recognised immediately.

What is it that gives the V-twin its magic? After all there have been many motorcycles that have been faster, more expensive, more exclusive, more powerful or more unusual. The answer lies somewhere between technology and emotion, which are uniquely fused in motorcycles and motorcycling. Few motorcycle enthusiasts are interested only in technology and engineering – there are plenty of other machines which are just as technically interesting and a lot easier and cleaner to work on, as any collector of clocks or cameras can testify – equally few are truly indifferent to the mechanical aspects of their mounts. Even if they do not know a torque wrench from a Stillson wrench, they are still likely to be interested in what goes on under those shiny aluminium covers, and to lard their conversation with references to brake horse power, torque, and overhead cam shafts.

The V-twin is different things to different people.

Firstly, there is the sheer heritage of the design. V-twin engines were one of the earliest (and most effective) ways of squeezing more power into a motorcycle frame, and they were winning races before World War One. Who with an interest in bikes could forget the 1911 Senior TT when the Indian team came in first, second and third, and shattered British complacency? And what about the Brough Superior, guaranteed in writing to reach 100 mph in 1925? Broughs were, of course, the favoured mount of TE Lawrence,

Moto-Guzzi 500cc Bicylindrica racer, 1935.

12

better known as Lawrence of Arabia, who once raced a Bristol fighter with his Brough and won (he also died on a Brough). Then there was Rollie Free, who wore only swimming trunks and tennis shoes as he rode a Vincent record-breaker at more than 150 mph, a record-breaker which later went into production as the Black Lightning. And – seemingly forever – there has been the Harley-Davidson, for many people the epitome of what a motorcycle should be: big, strong, powerful and virtually indestructible, the Freedom Machine.

Secondly, there is the elegance of the V-twin. In engineering, as in mathematics, 'elegance' does not mean luxury or styling. It means the simplest and best solution to a given problem. It is far easier to recognise than to define, but the V-twin has it. The centre of gravity is low, so that the motorcycle is 'flickable' at speed but is also easy to drive at a walking pace or even to manhandle. The V-twin is narrow, which makes it easily manoeuvrable in tight spaces, including urban traffic: the engine fits neatly in the frame, wasting no space and well protected in the event of a spill: and the power which can now be extracted from a well-designed one-litre twin is adequate for anyone, 70–80 bhp at the least, and 90 bhp or more without seriously impairing reliability. Of course, in the past the power outputs were lower than this, but they were still well ahead of any of the competition, and machines like the Brough Superior New SS100 can still give many modern superbikes a run for their money.

Thirdly, the engine is relatively simple. In one way this is another aspect of the question of elegance, but it also has several practical consequences. The most immediate is that the engine is readily comprehensible to the average mechanic, who does not need a degree in engineering to work on it or (within reason) a forest of special tools and factory training, though the Japanese are doing their best to change this in their latest designs. Furthermore, as already mentioned, you are unlikely to do any very serious damage (at least to the motorcycle) if you do throw it down the road. Compare the V-twin in this respect with a typical Japanese transverse four, with its alternator mounted on the end of the crankshaft: anything more than the slightest fall stands an excellent chance of destroying the alternator, and quite possibly bending the crankshaft as well.

Finally, the whole configuration looks and sounds right. This is not just a matter of aesthetics: there is an old engineering saying that if it looks right then it probably is right. You can *see* when something is overcomplicated, top-heavy or awkwardly proportioned; and the V-twin is not. It is true, though, that there have been other engine layouts which also have their fanatical devotees, and it is worth comparing these with the V-twin in order to see their attractions and drawbacks.

Foremost, there is the single. Famous machines such as the double-knocker Norton, the Velocette 350cc and 500cc singles, the four-valve Rudges and the AJS 7R 'Boy's Racer' are magnificent motorcycles in anyone's book. Their problem is that a point comes where if you want more power you also need more cylinders. At about 500cc, the sheer size of the piston and of all the ancillaries – con-rods, valves, push-rods and rocker-arms – grows so great that vibration becomes spectacular, and you start running into difficulties in revving the engine fast enough, because the entire reciprocating mass has to be arrested four times for each power stroke – twice at top dead centre, and twice at bottom dead centre – and its direction of motion reversed. You can overcome problems with the weight of the valve train by using overhead cams. You can remove valve float (or at least make sure that it occurs at a much higher speed) by going to a four-valve head and, of course, you can try desmodromic valve control as described later in the chapter on Ducati, but there is still the problem of that increasingly massive piston, because the weight of the piston increases as the cube of its radius while the swept volume increases only as the square.

What is more, the four-stroke single fires only once in every two revolutions, so although the power comes in large lumps it does not come smoothly. This imposes a considerable strain on the moving parts, as well as causing additional vibration, and means that if you want to smooth things out you will need to use either a large flywheel (which reduces the responsiveness of the bike), or to run the motor so fast that the vibration becomes a buzz, practical with a very small engine but not much use at anything over 125cc. Alternatively you can either learn to live with it (which is the traditional approach), or else use the universal Japanese balance shaft, at which point you lose sight of the simplicity and elegance which was the original attraction of the single, and might as well build a multi-cylinder engine.

The parallel twin is the next logical step and has several advantages. It is simple and cheap to make and, even though there are two pistons instead of one, the cube/square relationship mentioned above means that the reciprocating masses need not be any greater. And because there is a power stroke on every revolution, power delivery is twice as evenly spread as in a single, so the result is a smoother, more powerful, more tractable engine. The success of the parallel twin was, however, largely due to one superb design – the Triumph Speed Twin – which everyone else copied, and which lost some of its original charm in the process. The Speed Twin was a 500cc motorcycle and it was a revelation, but it became increasingly rough when the capacity was increased in the search for more power. It was still very acceptable at 650cc, but at 750cc the vibrations became very noticeable indeed, and the 828cc Norton Commando really needed the rubber mounts which isolated the motor from the frame.

Another possible layout for a twin-cylinder engine is the flat twin, as used transversely in BMWs and post-1935 Douglases, or in line in older Douggies, in the original Broughs and in many other vintage machines. Looked at dispassionately, the flat twin is very similar to a V-twin: in fact, it is the limiting case of a V-twin, with 180° between the cylinders. For this reason, I have included the flat twin in this book, and we shall come back to it later.

Any greater number of cylinders brings with it one enormous difficulty,

Beaumont Radial. It is unlikely that this machine was ever built: the three cylinder Beaumont engine was also scheduled to appear in a three-wheeler. It dates from the early 1940s.

cooling. Either you run the engine transversely across the frame, which makes for a ridiculously wide motorcycle with a very high centre of gravity (which may still have cooling problems), or you use liquid cooling. It is true that there have been four-cylinder engines which have not been mounted transversely and which have not been liquid cooled, but these have either been sufficiently low powered (and hence cool running) that cooling them has been no problem, or else they have been notorious for cooling problems. The Henderson, the Nimbus and the FN are examples of the former; the Ariel Square Four (the 'Squariel') and the AJS V4 'Porcupine' are classic examples of the latter. The 'Porcupine' was so named because of its spiky head finning, which was still inadequate to shed heat as fast as it was needed. The designers seriously considered casting the heads in solid silver, to improve heat transfer, until they found out the tensile strength of silver and what the weight penalty would be.

There is, of course, nothing inherently wrong with liquid cooling – it has, after all, been used in cars and racing bikes for years – but it does add weight and complexity, which are two things that any machine (and especially any motorcycle) can live without. It also tends to raise the centre of gravity, because there has to be a large and fairly heavy radiator somewhere at the front of the bike and, in order to preserve a reasonable wheelbase, the usual place is up in front of the cylinders. The best liquid-cooled designs are probably the flat four, as found in the Honda Goldwing, and the four-on-its-side, as first tried out by Ariel and finally put into production in the BMW K-series. And the best motorcycle with more than two air-cooled cylinders is probably the 120°-crank Laverda triple, though devotees of the original Jota have a valid point and Triumph Trident owners will also have something to say.

The more attentive reader may have noticed that I have, so far, made no mention of two-strokes. The reason for this is that two strokes are usually of

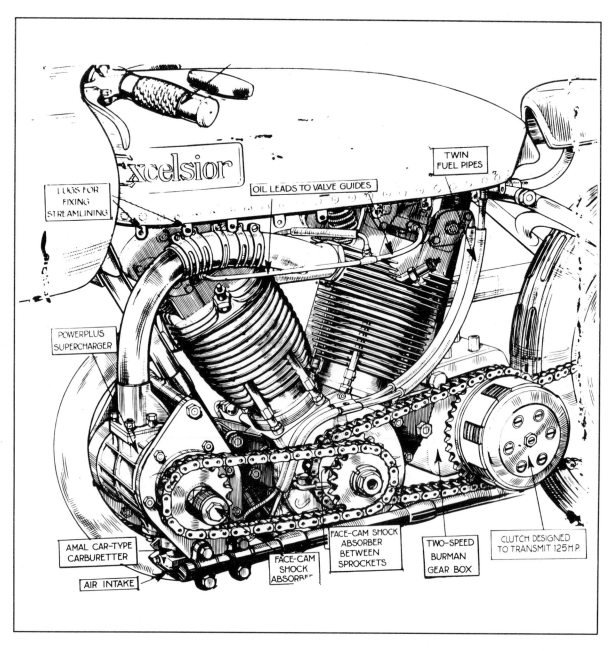

LUGS FOR FIXING STREAMLINING

OIL LEADS TO VALVE GUIDES

TWIN FUEL PIPES

POWERPLUS SUPERCHARGER

AMAL CAR-TYPE CARBURETTER

AIR INTAKE

FACE-CAM SHOCK ABSORBER

FACE-CAM SHOCK ABSORBER BETWEEN SPROCKETS

TWO-SPEED BURMAN GEAR BOX

CLUTCH DESIGNED TO TRANSMIT 125 H.P.

a far lower thermal efficiency than four-strokes (though often of a higher volumetric efficiency), which means that a big two-stroke tends to guzzle fuel at a rate which rules it out from serious consideration. It is also very difficult to design an efficient two-stroke cylinder with a volume significantly greater than 250cc, because of problems with the exhaust gases and the incoming charge mixing, which mean that multi-cylinder engines are essential if you want real power. There have, however, been a few two-stroke V-twins, such as the Stanger and WAG (in Britain) and the Ercolli-Cavallone (in Italy). All three flourished for brief periods in the 1920s, but the two-stroke V-twin has

The blown Excelsior in this 50 year old artwork dates from 1931. Although it was the heart of the depression, many manufacturers released 'concept bikes' to encourage the buyers of their bread-and-butter 'depression specials'.

Husquarna TT bike, 1935 (above and right). After a quayside disaster in Sweden, when the bikes were dropped by a crane, runners were assembled from the wreckage – but did not do very well.

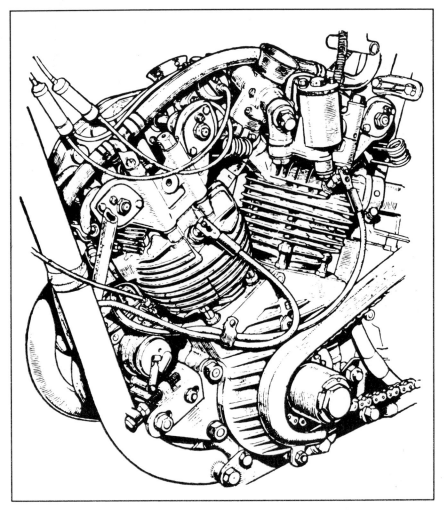

never been a serious contender as a motorcycle engine. There have been a few more two-stroke flat twins, including a BMW prototype after the last war, but once again these were not a part of the mainstream of motorcycle design, and cannot really be called 'classics'.

To return to the V-twin, it is a layout with many advantages. Not only does it pack a good deal of swept volume, and hence plenty of power (especially torque) into a compact space, it is also fairly easy to cool (very easy to cool at 90° and beyond), easy to balance in such a way as to get rid of the worst vibration, and capable of being taken up to 1000 cc with impunity, and beyond if necessary. One other advantage – which we are inclined to forget nowadays – is that a V-twin is virtually two singles on a common crank-case: if one fails, the other will get you home. It was not that early engines were particularly unreliable *per se*, for the fault usually lay with their owners, whose mechanical experience might (or might not) extend to a pedal cycle or a sewing machine, but to whom ideas such as maintenance and lubrication were often distinctly unclear if not downright foreign. In those early days a large swept volume was essential. Compression ratios might be as low as $2\frac{1}{2}$:1, and inlet valves were usually of the 'automatic' variety, which means they were sucked open by the falling piston, against a very weak spring. To make matters worse, after gearboxes were introduced, people disliked changing gear any more than was strictly necessary, and a motorcycle which could go everywhere in 'top speed' was highly prized. By designing a big engine with a wide spread of torque, especially at the lower end of the rev range (the famous low-speed 'grunt' of the V-twin), it was possible to make a motorcycle which could crawl through muddy tracks or clinging sand, or cross rutted and bumpy paths at a walking pace, and then barrel along the open road at fifty miles an hour or more.

One of the most fundamental design variables in a V-twin is the included angle between the cylinders; so much nonsense is talked about this that it is worth examining the problem in some detail. Included angles have varied from 26°, in the 1929 Matchless Silver Arrow, to 120° in the Moto-Guzzi Bicilindrica racer of 1935 and to 180° if, as I have done, you count the flat twin as a form of vee. The vast majority, though, have been either 90° or in the 45–55° range.

The 90° V-twin is perhaps the most obvious design, and it has several advantages. One of the easiest to see is that the cylinders are well separated for cooling; another is that there is plenty of room for fitting carburettors and exhaust pipes; and a third is that it is easy to balance the primary forces caused by the rise and fall of the pistons by adding a counterweight equal to the weight of one piston plus the small end. Achieving secondary balance is more of a problem, because there is an irreducible and powerful secondary vibration at twice engine speed, acting at right angles to a line bisecting the cylinder angle but, if the engine is conventionally mounted, this is acting in the least noticeable plane, namely in line with the direction of motion of the motorcycle. This secondary vibration is really only noticeable when you are dealing with a big engine, but then most V-twins have traditionally been big.

Moto-Guzzi 850, 1984.

18

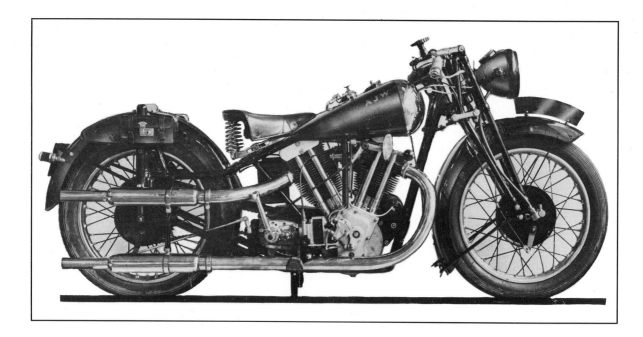

The 90° engine does, however, have its drawbacks. If 'balance' is taken to include the firing interval – which strictly it does not, but practically it does – then a 90° twin with a conventional single-throw crankshaft suffers from a certain lack of balance in this department. The shorter firing interval is 270°, or three-quarters of a revolution, and the longer one is 450°, or one and a quarter revolutions. This accounts for the characteristic 'beat' of the exhaust note, but means that we are back to considering flywheels, though they need not be anything like as large as on a single. It also accounts for the way in which V-twins have to be kick-started: you have to begin with the correct cylinder, in order to get a good long swing. (As an aside, one of the reasons why modern V-twins usually rely solely on an 'electric foot', rather than supplying a kick-start as well, is that a 1000 cc engine with a compression ratio in excess of 9:1 would be all but impossible to start: a Vincent is hard enough and the Shadow is only 7.3:1.)

The 90° V-twin is also something of a problem to mount in the frame. Conventional mounting, with the cylinders arranged more-or-less symmetrically about the vertical axis, is quite possible, but there is an odd-looking space in the middle and the wheelbase can get quite long. And because 90° V-twins have mostly been 'no compromise' sporting engines, rear cylinder cooling is not particularly brilliant. The alternative, pioneered by Ducati, is to tilt the engine in the frame, so that the front cylinder points more-or-less forward, and the rear cylinder is more-or-less vertical. This allows excellent cooling, and is the path also adopted by Hesketh, but it does have the disadvantage (especially with an overhead cam engine) that the seat height is necessarily forced up. The secondary vibration already mentioned also has a vertical and a fore-and-aft component, instead of just fore-and-aft, although this is relatively minor and need not cause any concern. There is a fair objection that this sort of mounting looks a bit odd, though presumably less so to Italians who are used to 'flat singles' in the Moto-Guzzi mould, with one cylinder pointing straight forward.

Moto-Guzzi, of course, mount their 90° V-twin transversely. The difficulties here are the secondary vibration already mentioned, which is now from side to side instead of fore-and-aft, which makes it much more noticeable and harder to control, and the fact that the cylinders tend to get in the way of the rider's knees; we shall return to these and other drawbacks in Chapter 8.

Because of the drawbacks of the 90° V-twin, and because cooling the lower-powered motors of the past was less of a problem, the traditonal included angle of a V-twin was around 45°, though larger angles for production expediency have been quite common: the Vincent Series A Rapide was 47.5°, and the later models were 50°.

At anything around this configuration, the firing intervals are rather more even (315° and 405° for a 45° Vee), and a counterbalance of around 35% of the total reciprocating weight gives satisfactory smoothness without, however, the perfect primary balance of the 90° motor. On the other hand, the secondary imbalance is considerably reduced, and is made up of both a vertical and a horizontal component (assuming the Vee is mounted symmetrically about the vertical axis, in line with the frame), so it can easily be controlled with rubber engine mounts if need be. An additional advantage is that while one piston is at a dead-centre point (TDC or BDC) and thus

1932 Harley-Davidson 74 ci outfit. Huge box sidecars like these furnished an alternative to light vans, even as late as the 1950s. Note the mounting of the spare wheel.

reversing its direction, the other is travelling at nearly maximum velocity. This means that the kinetic energy stored in the pistons is much more nearly constant than with other configurations, especially those where the pistons reach their dead-centre points simultaneously, so the whole reciprocating mass contributes to the flywheel effect. The 45° engine also fits very neatly into the frame, with just enough room to fit exhausts and carburettors conveniently, and it cannot be denied that it looks superb; everything is visually in one piece, which must account in some measure for the continuing popularity of the Harley-Davidson. The only real drawback – and it is a serious one – is cooling. It is true that it is possible to extract more than 70 bhp from a 45° engine, but the full power of the engine is not usable for long periods or overheating becomes a serious problem. I suspect that the reason why the New SS100 was able to get away with its power was that there were very few places where it could be used; there were no motorways in those days (though Hitler's autobahns were under construction), and on

Power and glory – the way a Harley oughtta look

Brute power: a classic big V-twin motor in a 1920 Coventry Eagle.

the race-track no-one expected longevity. Similarly, most super-powerful Harley-Davidsons are used more for drag racing than for long-distance riding at high speeds.

There have also been various attempts to 'split the difference' between the 45° and 90° twins. One that is both simple and elegant is the Moto-Morini 72° twin. The nominal firing interval is 288°/432°, but because the cylinders are moved slightly apart to make room for the crankshaft, the cylinder axes meet slightly below the centre line of the crankshaft. This effect is technically known as *désaxé*, and has the effect that the intervals are a degree or so different. The advantage of the 72° layout is that it gives the improved cooling and accessibility of the wider angle, a fair compromise on both balance and firing interval, and an engine which fits nicely into the frame: looks and performance are thus blended into a very satisfactory package.

Recently the Japanese have been applying their own typically 'high-tech' solutions to the V-twin. There are two of these, namely the universal Japanese balance-shaft and the staggered crank. The former is technically uninteresting, and has appeared on countless other Japanese machines of varying configurations and sizes. The second is much more intriguing.

There have traditionally been two ways of making a V-twin crankshaft. They are both single-throw, but the difference lies in whether the cylinders are offset or not. In most modern designs, they are: the two con-rods run side-by-side which introduces a slight rocking couple and results in the cylinders being slightly offset, which incidentally helps the cooling of the rear cylinder. The older system is to have the two cylinders in line, which means that one of the con-rods has to be forked so that the other can run inside it, the so-called 'knife and fork' design. It makes for a tidy-looking engine and may have had its advantages in the past but it is heavy and expensive, does nothing for rear-cylinder cooling and has no particular advantage, apart from making the engine ever so slightly slimmer, and removing the rocking couple. Harley-Davidson engines are still of the 'knife and fork' variety to this day.

If the crankshaft is made with two throws, though, it is possible to alter the firing angles and balance without altering the included cylinder angle. This seems to have been first tried at the end of World War Two by George Brough, with a 90° twin, using a built-up three-flywheel crankshaft (the middle flywheel was between the two crank-pins). At the expense of a slightly greater (but still insignificant) rocking couple, this allowed the manufacture of an engine which combined several of the desirable characteristics of both narrow-angle and wide-angle twins. George Brough seems to have decided that there was no great advantage in this approach (but then, he was using it only in an attempt to control the firing angle), but Honda's VT500 appeared with a 52° included angle and a 76° effective angle. This provides similar advantages to the Morini 72° layout (actually slightly better balance, because the angle is nearer 90°), while still allowing an admirably compact engine. The VT500 is, of course, liquid cooled, because air cooling a high-performance 52° twin is simply not on nowadays.

Considering the other angles, we can dismiss both the ultra-narrow angle and the ultra-wide angle as evolutionary dead-ends of no particular significance: the 26° Matchless provided an admirably even firing angle but owes more to the vertical twin than to the V-twin, and the 120° Moto-Guzzi racer was a masterpiece of improvisation which was never seen on a production road-going motorcycle. Rather more important is the 180° Vee, or the flat twin.

This layout has several major advantages. Primary balance is perfect, for obvious reason; the centre of gravity can be very low indeed; accessibility is excellent; and unless the engine is mounted fore-and-aft cooling can hardly be bettered. There are, however, certain compensating disadvantages.

The first disadvantage is that, although firing is perfectly even, at 180° both pistons reach their dead-centre points simultaneously, so a good-sized flywheel is needed for maximum smoothness. Furthermore, as the swept volume climbs over about 750cc, there is a powerful side-to-side vibration caused by reaction to the power stroke: with the 900cc and 1000cc BMWs this manifests itself as a marked shake below about 2000–2500 rpm.

The second disadvantage is that the configuration makes for a wide (or long) engine, which inhibits fancy valve gear; overhead cams would add still more to the distance between the cam-box or rocker-box tops. Mounted in-line a long engine makes for a long wheelbase: mounted transversely, it

Not all classics are designed for the European market: Moto-Guzzi's California 2.

inhibits spirited cornering, though this is less of a problem than it might seem because most people run out of bravery shortly before a BMW runs out of clearance, and (as a matter of interest) the bits that occasionally ground on my R100RS are the prop-stand on left-handers and the brake-lever on right-handers.

The main fear which most people have, of damaging the cylinders in the event of a spill, is substantially unfounded, at least on a BMW. I once saw an R75/5 which had taken the rear axle out of a Ford Escort and put the rider in hospital for several months, but when he came out he only had to replace one rocker-box cover. He also replaced one head, mainly for cosmetic reasons, because a couple of fins were badly chipped. The last objection, that the cylinders get in the way of your feet, never seems to worry most people who ride flat twins, as distinct from armchair critics. A much more serious problem is that a leaky carburettor float bowl will piddle merrily on a rider's shoe!

2
The Great American Vee

No classic motorcycle can be talked about in wholly rational terms and whether or not the Harley-Davidson is the greatest of them all, as so many of its admirers believe, it is certainly one of the hardest to talk about dispassionately. According to your point of view, it is strong and rugged or crude and tractor-like: perfect for relaxed cruising, or too uncomfortable at speed for anything else: impressive, or just gross.

Tank decals on 1984 Harley-Davidsons: nostalgia all the way.

One thing that everyone agrees, though, is that it is almost impossible to be indifferent to a Harley. You either love them or loathe them. Like a lot else in motorcycling, this loving or loathing is not necessarily based on logic, or even on experience. Many of the keenest admirers of Harley-Davidsons have never sat astride one, let alone ridden one or owned one, and exactly the same is true of many of their keenest critics.

Evolution is the key word with Harley-Davidson; it's a word that the company themselves use a lot. With the exception of a few 'funnies', such as the fore-and-aft flat twins built from 1919 to 1922 (for no apparent reason) and the transverse flat twins built between 1941 and 1943 (for the US Army), their earliest V-twins derived from their still earlier singles, and everything since then has been an evolutionary development from there. The evolution has not always been that fast. Foot shifts waited until 1952, and rear suspension (at least on the top-of-the-line models) did not appear until 1956. Furthermore, because improvements were introduced as and when the gentlemen at Juneau Avenue, Milwaulkee, got around to them, it is not easy to divide the bikes into clear families. They would try out an innovation on one model before adding it to the others, which makes for a degree of overlap. For example, the smaller machines had sprung rear ends in 1952. On top of all this, old designs were also offered for a while – sometimes a long while – after new ones had been introduced, either as a lower-cost option or for some particular virtue that the old model had in greater quantities than the new; thus, the cheaper, simpler, even longer-lived, but rather lower-powered side-valve motors survived long after the 1936 introduction of overhead valves.

Perhaps the best approach is to follow as far as possible the custom of Harley devotees, and use the engine type. This gives us the *Seven Ages of Harley-Davidson*.

These are first, the very early days, before the V-twin: second, the 'teens and twenties, when Harley first made their name and then were badly shaken by the rise of the ultra-cheap Ford car: third, the period from 1929–1936, when the first modern-looking bikes appeared: fourth, the 'knucklehead' (overhead valve) era, 1936–47: fifth, the 'panhead' era (hydraulic lifters and

alloy heads), 1948–65: sixth, the 'shovelhead', a development of the 'pan-head', 1966–83: and seventh, the 'blockhead', introduced in 1984.

The original machine that started it all was a 25 cubic inch (410cc) belt-drive single, built in 1903 by three young friends: their names were Bill Harley, and Arthur and Walter Davidson. A friend admired it, and asked if they could build another like it. In 1904 they made two, one for the friend and another which found a ready sale. In 1905 there were eight more, and in 1906, Arthur and Walter's father built the lads a wooden shed ten feet by fifteen feet with HARLEY DAVIDSON MOTOR CO on the door, and they built fifty motorcycles. The 1906 model was a 35 ci (575cc) model, still with no clutch or gearbox, and it was a real family business – the Davidsons' Aunt Janet pin-striped the tanks and devised the company logo. In 1907, they made about 150 machines, that was the year they were joined by William A Davidson, the eldest brother, and formed a corporation. Meanwhile, Bill Harley decided to go to university and get a degree in automotive engineering.

Although they made about 450 motorcycles in 1908, the story really picks up in 1909 when Bill Harley came back from university long enough to design a V-twin. He did it in the standard way for the period, which was basically just to add a second cylinder to the existing single, and then beef up the bottom end to stand the extra power (hence the forked con-rod!). This was the Model 5D, with 49·5 ci (811cc) and 6½ horsepower, about a 50 per cent improvement on the singles. From then on, singles were strictly the second string in Milwaulkee, sold either for mundane transportation or (in the case of the famous 'peashooter') for racing. The V-twin had arrived to stay.

In their Second Age, Harley-Davidsons gained their reputation in two ways. One was by being virtually indestructible, which they had to be, given the state of American roads at the time and the fact that most of their riders were more used to horses than to machinery. The other was performance, especially in racing. The engine grew to 60.34 ci in 1912, the same year that a clutch was offered. Chain drive replaced belt in 1913, and 1914 saw a two-speed gearbox. In 1915, this grew to a three-speeder, and electric lighting was offered as well. In those days that put Harley-Davidson at the cutting edge of motorcycle design; and even the stock machine of the mid-teens could be pursuaded to hit the magic 'mile a minute', whilst still retaining the flexibility to chug and chuff along the most appalling tracks.

The racers of the time were, of course, still faster, and it was from the 'teens that the famous Harley-Davidson 'wrecking crew' took over from Indian, dominating the sport in the United States and doing surprisingly well in overseas events. After the war, racing successes were due to a combination of xenophobia, lack of foreign bikes, and downright dishonest AMA regulations which penalised innovation and efficiency but, in those heady days, Harleys could take on anyone on their own merits and stand a good chance of winning – though they never equalled Indian's 1–2–3 on the Island in 1911, though.

The blockhead.

The 1920s were not quite as 'roaring' as Milwaulkee might have liked. With Ford selling reliable four-wheelers for only $245 in 1920, a big, powerful, well-made motorcycle lacked the appeal it had in Europe (where it might well be attached to a side-car and used as family transport). This not only harmed sales, it also laid the foundations of the 'outlaw' image, because the puritan work ethic held that it was bad enough to buy a vehicle for fun rather than utility. To enjoy riding it as well was altogether too much!

Despite this, and despite the fact that they pulled out of racing in 1921 for financial reasons, the company introduced the first 74 ci (1213cc) Harley in 1922 – the first of a long, long line. Obviously, a 45° V-twin of such capacity was not lacking in torque; and the adoption of aluminium pistons and an inlet-over-exhaust valve system meant that it was not lacking in power, either. The nominal 9.5 horsepower tells nothing like the whole story: these were massive cart-horses at the very least, or perhaps a variety of racing elephant.

The 74-inch machine ran with few changes until 1929, though the market was hard: in 1926 the company even reintroduced a single. With a difficult home market, it was the overseas sales that kept the firm afloat. In 1921 there were Harley-Davidson dealers in 67 countries, a record which has not been broken since. For the most part the big twins were popular in backward countries, where simplicity and ruggedness were at a premium, and we may recall that much of 1920s America wasn't too far from this stage, either.

Our Third Age begins in 1929 with the classic 45 ci (actually 45.32, or 742cc). It was significant for two reasons. The first, that this was to be a standard engine size for many years to come; and the second, that it was the first modern-looking Harley. The saddle-tank look now broke away from the increasingly dated Harley appearance, even if there was still no rear suspension and only distinctly primitive front suspension. The 45 ci engine also powered the late-lamented Servicar three-wheeler from 1932 to 1974, which can still be seen now in Los Angeles (where the police still have a few), in Delhi (where they are used as taxis, though in most cases the faithful V-twin has been replaced with a monster single-cylinder diesel), and in all sorts of other unlikely places.

A 74-inch model – the VL – was introduced in 1930, to carry on the modern styling introduced on the 45-inch the previous year. This was, however, something of a disaster. Not everything used to break, but there were enough ill-considered parts that it sometimes seemed like it. The problem was not just the engine: the clutch was not man enough for the job; the mufflers (silencers) used to coke up and all but stop the bike; and the frames used to fracture. Apart from that – and a few other minor problems – they were fine, and they could hit 90 mph on a good day! They were rapidly and dramatically improved and became the definitive 'flathead' (side-valve) Harleys. They ran in parallel with the 45-inch machine, and with the $30\frac{1}{2}$-inch (500cc) single. The 61-inch dropped temporarily out of sight in 1929.

The Fourth Age is the first one of which the average modern rider will have experience. It began in 1936 with the all-OHV 'knucklehead' engine, first in 61-inch (actually 61.74, 1012cc) and then in 1941 in 74-inch capacities. With about 40 horsepower from the smaller machine and perhaps 45 (but *lots* more torque) from the bigger one, performance improved significantly. These are touted as the first of the 'modern' Harleys. The same year, though, also saw an 80-inch (1340cc) side-valve, a monster engine with the pulling power of a tractor. The 45-inch flathead remained, and so did the 74-inch side-valve, so there was no lack of choice! Unfortunately, although the 'knucklehead' was a runaway success, there were considerable problems with BMW's largest market and by the early 1940s Uncle Sam was accounting for a great deal of Harley-Davidson's production capacity. The machine they chose was the 45-inch WLA flathead, with a few additions such as a rifle scabbard beside the front forks and a 'bash plate' under the engine. These are now very sought after as collectors' pieces, though many readers will no doubt remember when they could still be bought in batches of a dozen or more for next to nothing. About 80,000 military 45-inch

1984 Tour-Glide.

machines were made, including about 20,000 WLC models for Canadian forces: these featured a hand clutch and foot change, the first models to be so equipped as a matter of course.

There is also a rare and unusual shaft-drive flat twin, the XA, which was obviously modelled on the BMW. Why the Army decided that it wanted them, when the proven WLA was already available, is a mystery. Only 1000 were made, which makes them very rare indeed.

Although the 80-inch sv machines died with the war in 1945, the knucklehead 61-inch and (rare) 74-inch model (which only hit production in 1941) soldiered on. So did the 45-inch flathead, with the first batch of 'civilian' models actually being de-militarised WLAs. It was not until 1948 that a new machine appeared, thus instigating the Fifth Age. It was simply the old machine with an improved engine, a 61-inch or 74-inch alloy-headed development of the 'knucklehead'. This rapidly became known as the 'panhead', and it is not hard to see why: the rocker-box covers do have a

The classic iron flathead.

distinctly culinary look to them. In 1949, another major innovation (at least for Harley-Davidson) appeared: hydraulic front forks. These were by no means unusual elsewhere – BMWs had them as early as 1938 – but they were the first step in modernising a machine which was by now beginning to look distinctly vintage.

The next submission to modernity, fifteen to twenty years after most other manufacturers, was the adoption in 1952 of hand clutches and foot shifts though – to be fair – there had been a 'hill start lever' (or 'very heavy manual clutch') option for several years before that, fitted in addition to the foot clutch and retaining the hand change. Even after 1952, manual shift/foot clutch continued to be an option and was theoretically available into the 1980s.

In 1952 the first sprung-tail Harley appeared. This was not too far behind the times, though many of the more expensive or advanced European machines had again preceded it by a decade and a half, but it was confined to the Model K. This was a development of the faithful old 45-inch bike, with an alternative 55-inch (900cc) option. The 61-inch and 74-inch 'real' Harleys waited until 1958, when they became the Duo-Glide models. Thus, in 1957, it was still possible to buy a rigid-framed, foot-clutch, hand-shift motor-cycle, though if you wanted side-valves, you had either to put up with a

32

One of the best toyshops in England: Three Cross Motorcycles, Harley-Davidson dealers.

sprung rear end or transplant a new 45-inch (or pre-1948) engine into a Hydra-Glide frame.

The 1950s machines still had very leisurely performance for such big motorcycles, and the handling was not impressive either. Fortunately, drag-racing was more the American sporting scene than bend-swinging, and the torquey low-geared Harley-Davidson was as well-suited to the former as it was ill-suited to the latter. This was dramatically confirmed by the XL series, first introduced in 1957.

The original 55-inch (actually 53.9 ci, 883cc) engine delivered a modest enough 40 bhp, but 1958 saw a higher compression ratio, better breathing and a lightened valve-train. 1959 completed the transformation with 'hotter' cams. The engine was in unit with the gearbox, and substitution of new-fangled light alloy for such things as engine mountings meant that the bike was, by Harley-Davidson standards, quite light. Certainly, the 1959 XLCH could not be faulted for top speed (110–120 mph) or acceleration (13-second standing quarters), and it became one of the all-time classics. The fearful vibration at anything much over 60 mph and the still-stodgy cornering were forgiven: this was *the* dragster Harley.

The XL series and the panheads co-existed until 1965, the year in which the Duo-Glide acquired electric starting and became the Electra-Glide. In 1966 came the 'shovelhead' version of the 74-inch motor, along with an 80-inch (1340cc) variant: they both owed a great deal to the 'panhead', and a certain amount to the XL series (though they were still resolutely non unit-construction), and the power was up again. The FLH high-compression model delivered about 60 bhp, and the 'cooking' FL about 54 bhp, the same as Triumph extracted from a 750cc parallel twin and used to drive a motorcycle anything up to 200 1b lighter!

The shovelhead marked the beginning of the Sixth Age, in which Harley-Davidson realised that motorcycling in the United States was now as much a part of the 'leisure industry' as a sport for enthusiasts. The 1960s and 1970s saw a proliferation of models, each aimed at a very specialised part of the market: the all-round motorcycle was rapidly losing ground. Apart from those who did not really care what sort of motor-cycle they had, as long as it was a Harley-Davidson, the market is now divided into three parts.

The first is the touring market. In American parlance this means a vast machine, laden with luggage and accessories, designed to be ridden at comparatively low speeds for very long distances on straight roads. Some-thing like the monstrous Tour-Glide is well suited for this, but finds itself in difficulties on winding Alpine roads or little, rural dirt-tracks, to say nothing of European traffic. Such a machine really does approach the old gibe about a two-wheeled motor car.

The second is the sporting market. As we have already suggested, this is aimed at the drag-racer. Handling on the newer Harleys, although vastly better than the touring machines and older Harleys, is still a long way behind the best of the Europeans. But, of course, there is not the need for handling in most of the United States that there is in Europe. In most of the States you

1984 Blockhead – allegedly a sporting motorcycle!

really have to go looking for twisty bits. Nevertheless, there are places where handling is appreciated – in the canyons outside Los Angeles, for example – and it is also here that Nortons, Velocettes and other machines with smaller engines, lighter frames and superior handling are prized most highly.

The third sector of the market is more concerned with looks than with anything else. Such machines are epitomised by the fully-chopped hardtails, with over-extended front forks and negligible front brakes, but there have also been many 'factory customs' which pay more attention to looks than to riding practicality. In some cases, the people who buy these bikes even think of themselves as sporting riders – which leads us directly to the XLCR cafe racer.

A 'cafe racer', traditionally, is a machine tricked out to look like a racer but which is used for nothing more onerous than a blast to a favourite meeting place, traditionally the Ace Cafe. In the English idiom, the bike is a lean and purposeful Triton with a huge light-alloy tank and rearsets. In 1974, Harley-

Opposite:
Servi-Car – the faithful 45-inch flathead was always the power unit for the H-D three-wheeler ...

... except in Delhi, where enterprising Sardarji fitted 8-hp hand-start diesels when the Harley engine wore out (opposite below).

Right:
The Army-model WLC Harley-Davidsons provided reading and riding material – and a 65 mph advisory limit for the brave.

Davidson showed their XLCR as a styling exercise, and in 1977 they manufactured it.

With an XL engine in its 61-inch guise (it grew in 1972), the XLCR is a mean, moody, all-black machine that looks just about perfect. At 520 lb, it is light for a Harley but heavy for just about anything else, and 61 bhp is not really very impressive. For comparison, at that time 'staid' BMW could offer the R100RS with a 50 lb weight saving and 9 more bhp. On the other hand, the Harley's torque could give 13-second standing quarters, and it looked so good that innumerable poseurs who would never dream of using the performance bought it anyway. If the Ace Cafe were any further away than the end of a quarter-mile straight then the Triton owner would get there weeks ahead of the XLCR, but who would turn more heads when he (eventually) arrived?

The advantage of a model range that embraces three such disparate requirements is that by selecting the mix of ingredients carefully it is possible to build a motorcycle that will suit just about anyone, except perhaps the devotee of lightweights. This could be seen very clearly at the time of writing, when Harley-Davidson were just entering upon their Seventh Age.

The passage of the Seventh Age is marked by the introduction of yet another variant on the big old 45° V-twin, the 80-inch 'blockhead'. With a new all-alloy top end, lightened valve train (still with hydraulic lifters!), $8\frac{1}{2}:1$ compression ratio and lumpier cams, there is about 71 bhp on tap.

What the new engine meant, though, was that there were no fewer than fourteen models in the 1984 line-up, with a mixture of 80-inch blockheads, 80-inch shovelheads (the 74-inch was allowed to fade in the late 1970s), and 61-inch Sportsters derived from the XL series.

Although several models in the range are almost grotesque, such as the 762 lb FLHTC tourer, this unique combination of variety-through-similarity sums up the attraction of the Harley-Davidson. Its detractors may quote the old saying that 'in the United States you can sell 10,000 of *any-thing*', but as Harley-Davidson themselves put it, 'Anything else is less' . . . so why do they survive?

To begin with, a Harley is different. Different from other motorcycles, and even more different from cars. It symbolises the ability to stand alone, to travel, not to rely on other people. It is freedom, it is speed, it is power and it is a dream. It is all the things that only motorcyclists, and perhaps aviators, understand.

Also – and by no means unrelatedly – a Harley is understandable. Let other manufacturers boast that their machines are designed and built by robots: that just means that people need a robot, and a machine shop, and a degree in engineering and a forest of special tools just to work on them. Anyone with a bit of mechanical ability can understand and repair a Harley, which takes us back to self-reliance and freedom again.

A Harley will last half way to forever. The engine is big, a bit crude and rather old fashioned, and a little down on power compared with some would-

be competitors (though how much power can you use after 70 bhp?), but stand a new Harley next to some Oriental wonder and think about where they will be in ten, twenty or even fifty years. There is always a pleasure in owning something built to last.

A Harley looks and sounds like a motorcycle. We each have our own ideas of how a motorcycle should look – and we all agree that a Harley fits into that picture, even if the impression is a trifle vintage. Even those who would never ride one have to admit that there is not much to compare with the sound of that engine.

Finally, a Harley is not sold as a mere means of transport. It is sold as fun. And whether you get your fun barrelling through the canyons just after dawn, listening to the engine note booming back at you; whether you get your fun from travelling long distances at speeds which still allow you to appreciate the countryside; whether you regard a motor-cycle as a form of sculpture, a piece of art with handlebars and wheels; or whether you just like to sit around with a few friends, a few beers and a few classic motorcycles in the background after a good ride, somewhere there is a Harley that will fit the dream.

3
Indians and Others

Indian Brave, 1939. The timing side. See page 51 for other side.

Everyone knows the name of Harley-Davidson, but unless you were brought up on the great names of the American motorcycle industry, it is easy to forget that there was a time, long ago, when American V-twins ruled the world. For speed, technical innovation and handling they could compete with anyone and beat most. It was, however, a very long time ago. The highly esteemed Pope existed only from 1911 to 1918, the pioneering Thor ceased to be built in 1916, the improbably named Flying Merkel lasted from 1909 to 1915, while the very advanced overhead cam Cyclone was only made from 1913 to 1917 and Excelsior (a part of the Schwinn bicycle concern) made their last motorcycles in 1931 – though by that time their V-twins were known as Super-X, the name under which they had always been sold in England – because of a conflict with the Birmingham-based Excelsior concern. And then there was always the Crocker . . .

The other great name, though, in American V-twins is unquestionably Indian. Founded by Carl Oscar Hedstrom and George M Hendee in 1901, two years earlier than Harley-Davidson, the Hendee Manufacturing Company made their first Indian V-twin in 1905, though it was not offered as a production model until 1906. It featured a 26 ci, (426cc) 42° engine, with automatic inlet valves, mounted very high in the frame and still visibly owed a great deal to the pedal-cycle, but it was the ancestor of some very potent and impressive motorcycles.

It was also equipped with twistgrip controls, though they were a little unconventional by modern standards, with the throttle on the left and the advance/retard on the right.

With all-chain drive, the Indian was one of the most advanced machines on the road in 1906, but the 1907 model was even more impressive. Both inlet and exhaust valves were mechanically operated – though there was an air option for those who distrusted modern high technology – primary drive was by gear (and secondary still by chain, in an era of belt-drives), and with a weight of 135 lb (120 lb stripped for speed), the 38.61 ci (632cc) engine could propel the whole plot at up to 60 mph, depending on the final (fixed) gearing selected. Then, in 1909, the frame was redesigned to place the motor much lower, and two 42° V-twins, with all valves mechanically operated, were offered: the 61 ci (1000cc) Big Twin, and the 38 ci Light Twin.

Technical advance continued rapidly, with the 1910 models being offered with a two-speed gearbox and 'free engine' (clutch) as well as an engine-driven positive lubrication system. A kick-start did not appear until 1911, a momentous year in Indian history when the red machines from Springfield scooped first, second and third place in the five-year-old Isle of Man Tourist Trophy, run for the first time over the arduous Mountain Circuit.

The following year saw the development of the famous Indian spring frame, a major advance, and one which many manufacturers (including Harley-Davidson) were not to emulate for decades. Though it must be said that the frame design did not always keep the rear wheel precisely where it should have been (especially over rough terrain and with spirited driving), so the long continuation of the lighter and cheaper rigid frame alternative is no great surprise. The new frame was offered to the public in 1913, along with a considerably less successful innovation, electric starting. The batteries of the time were simply not up to it, and indeed were hard put to last long enough to give reliable lighting and (believe it or not) signalling.

With nearly 32,000 Indians manufactured in 1913, two machines out of every five manufactured that year in the United States were Indians – an impressive achievement.

Unfortunately for Indian, Harley-Davidson now decided to concentrate on competition successes as a means of publicising their motorcycles and there was more than a trace of fatal complacency in the older company, which was first shaken and then destroyed, as the Harley-Davidson 'wrecking crew' took more and more laurels. It also seems that there was a good deal of political wrangling inside the Indian company; Hedstrom resigned in

Indian 74 ci, 1927.

1913 and Hendee, the president of the company, took less and less interest in the day-to-day running of the firm. It seems likely that there was a major conflict between the accountants who saw everything in dollars and cents, and the enthusiasts who were more concerned with building motorcycles. Obviously, there has to be a commitment to profit within a company, but equally obviously you cannot expect a man who is only interested in accountancy to understand or care what makes a good motorcycle. This problem was to dog Indian all their days, as we shall see.

Nevertheless, the 1914 and 1915 models continued the Indian tradition of technical innovation combined with proven reliability. By 1915, the twins were made in 61-inch (1000cc) and 42-inch (688cc) sizes, with two speed gearboxes as standard and three speeds (based on a design by Hedstrom before he left the factory) as an option. Paradoxically to modern eyes, however, the 1915 models were equipped with side valves instead of overhead, and they developed more power, with 16-17 horsepower on the brake. A Splitdorf magneto/dynamo provided electric lighting and horn as

well as a spark, and if the battery failed (which was by no means improbable), direct lighting could be switched in. The famous 'Cannonball' Baker used one of these new Powerplus engines in a 1914 two-speed frame to make the Three Flags run from Vancouver to Tijuana: 1,655 miles in just over 81 hours elapsed time, a remarkable achievement in view of the almost non-existent roads of the period.

The war in Europe was making itself felt in the United States and, as we saw at the beginning of this chapter, one of the results was the disappearance of many of the smaller companies. Another result was the decision at Indian to concentrate on government orders, a short-sighted policy which risked the loyalty of established civilian customers and all but encouraged major dealers to go over to other makes who continued to service their civilian customers, even though (with classic accountants' thinking) the policy allowed Indian to produce and sell large numbers of motorcycles without any advertising or marketing expenses. In fact, this policy was not even a success in the short term, because poor accounting meant that the 20,000 machines, contracted to the government at $187.50 each, were actually sold at a loss. The War Department Indian was a 3-speed 61-inch machine, differing little – except for gear ratios and finish – from the civilian model. In 1918 a second contract was negotiated for a further 25,000 machines, this time at a price which allowed a modest profit but, for all that 40,000 plus

In keeping with their high price, Indians normally had expensive accessories, like this Bonniksen synchronous speedometer.

44

The drive to the Bonniksen clock.

Indians were delivered to Uncle Sam, the revenue which they generated was not enough to offset Indian's loss of credibility in the market place.

The war also saw the production of an in-line flat twin, the Model O of 1917. With a capacity of only 15 ci (246cc) it was an attempt to gain a foothold in the lightweight market. The design owed a great deal to the Douglas which was, at that time, doing sterling service at the front in Europe, but this new bike was little more successful than Indian's previous attempt at this market, which was a 13.5 ci (221cc) two-stroke in 1914.

Post-war production saw the resumption of the 61-inch twins, an enlarged 74-inch (1213cc) version for sidecar enthusiasts and the new Indian Scout, powered by what amounted to a 37-inch (606cc) version of the side-valve Powerplus engine. With geared primary drive and chain final drive the engine delivered about 12 horsepower on the brake, and a three-speed gearbox allowed easy hill climbing together with a top speed comfortably in excess of 50 mph.

The Scout was a real winner. Appreciably lighter and easier to manoeuvre (and especially to manhandle!) than the bigger twins, it rapidly became a favourite with law enforcement agencies. Even so, the 1920s were far from easy for the American motorcycle industry, and Indian were losing money: just under a million dollars in 1921, and well over a million in 1922, the year in which they introduced the Indian Chief. Export demand was buoyant, however, and more than one manufacturer paid Indian the most sincere compliment of all, even if one of the least welcome for any manufacturer, outright copying. One Japanese replica, it is said, even reproduced the US patent numbers! But the overall prospects were not good and the only realistic approach was to undertake another reorganisation, which this time took into account the fact that the motorcycle industry was declining. By reducing the workforce and restructuring production, the company actually managed in 1923 to turn in a modest profit (just over $200,000 on a turnover of $2.6 million).

In the course of this reorganisation, the company changed its name from the Hendee Manfacturing Company to the Indian Motocycle Company (the use of the odd word 'Motocycle' is said to have been in order to avoid patent actions) and went public; things definitely looked set to improve. Both the Scout and the Chief acquired Ricardo-type detachable heads for more efficient breathing in 1926, and the Scout was upped to 45 ci (737cc) in 1927 in response to Excelsior's success with a 50° V-twin of this capacity. The 45-inch machine was only very slightly heavier than the 37-inch model, but significantly more powerful, which made it an immediate success. It was also at this time that someone worked out that by replacing the Scout bottom end with a pair of turned-down Chief flywheels, a longer-stroke engine with a 57 ci (934cc) displacement could be created. Piston wear with the necessarily shortened pistons was a problem – 10,000 miles was a fair life – but the increase in power was noticeable and, if in the course of the rebuild the motor was 'blueprinted' and polished, the 'Stroker Scout' could genuinely compete against many 74-inch motorcycles.

Once again, a staggeringly bad decision by the accountants crippled Indian. Reasoning that motorcycle production was now stagnant, they refused to sanction any investment in tooling (which was by now very old

Opposite:
Indians were always beautifully finished, but in 1939 you could buy a cheap V-8 car for the price of a 4-cylinder Indian.

The speedometer was a proprietary accessory, but the Indian ammeter was a factory fitment.

and tired), and the president of the company, Frank Wechsler, resigned in protest in 1927. He had been with the company since 1905 and had effectively been running it since 1916, and it was he who had been responsible for the dramatic turnaround in the company's fortunes in 1923.

In 1928, the Scout was still further improved to give the so-called Model 101, generally agreed to be one of the best motorcycles of all time, A 370 1b motorcycle propelled by only 21 bhp may not seem like much nowadays but by the standards of the late 1920s it was very quick indeed, and the handling was superb. As supplied, it was good for well over 70 mph, and with a little judicious 'breathing upon' it could be induced to hit the magic 100 mph. Of course, these figures were for the 45-inch model, and as the 37-inch model was only slightly cheaper, it found little sale in competition with its bigger brother and was finally dropped in 1930. At the end of the 1920s the Indians, one by one, acquired front brakes, though these were and still are regarded with suspicion by many American riders to this day; the belief that using the front brakes too enthusiastically will throw you over the handlebars dies hard.

Like Harley-Davidson, Indian also flirted with three-wheelers, but never took them very seriously. A prototype based on the 101 appeared in 1931 under the unlikely title of the Indian Despatch Tow, which after a very brief

This 1913 Pope was one of the many first-class pre-World War One motorcycles made in the United States, before Indian and Harley-Davidson came to dominate the market.

48

No crash helmet and a 74 ci four – picture from the Indian catalogue of 1932.

production run disappeared in 1932, only to reappear as a Chief-based Package Car in 1935. The Package Car was available only to special order, and by the time it was discontinued at the beginning of the war it is likely that only a couple of hundred had been produced.

Although they refused to put any more money into motorcycles, the accountants became involved in more and more bizarre and ill-fated diversifications, including dropping a quarter of a million dollars on manufacturing a motor-car shock absorber which didn't work, a V-twin powered light car, and a prototype of a refrigerator which may never have been meant to work but which might boost the value of Indian stock when it became known that the company was diversifying . . . times were not good. In mid-1929 the company was reorganised yet again – this time with the intention of diversifying into aero engines – but within a couple of months the company was all but bankrupt, unable even to meet its payroll. Machines were offered to dealers only on condition that they paid on delivery, and Indian looked set to go under. Fortunately Hap Alzina, a leading dealer, managed to borrow enough money on short-term loans to bail out the company, but unfortunately the financial wheelings and dealings of the board continued to be as muddled as ever, until the company came under the control of E Paul Du Pont in 1930.

Although this provided a stable hand at the financial helm, technical advance now slowed still further. At long last, dry sump lubrication arrived in 1932 on the Motoplane, a derivative of the 45-inch 101 (previous models had been total-loss). A 30.5 ci (500cc) sleeved-down model of the same engine was also produced for the 'Junior Scout'. In 1933 there was yet another reorganisation, and over the next couple of years much of Indian's production machinery was sold off. The company was dying on its feet. There were, however, some improvements. One was the option of a 4-speed shift in 1934; another was the introduction of the new 1935 45-inch Sport Scout, owing a lot to the Motoplane and a good deal to English designs. The front forks were of girder type rather than the traditional Indian, and the wheelbase was only 56.5-inch, distinctly short by contemporary American standards. Also new for 1935 was the option of light alloy barrels and high-compression heads for the Chief and Super Scout, the Y type motor as distinct from the cast-iron G-type.

In 1940, the plunger rear frame was adopted (though it was far from perfect) but, by the 1942 model year, war production was once again absorbing the majority of Indian's production, in the form of the 30.5 ci 640. This was basically a Junior Scout/Scout hybrid with increased ground clearance for battlefield conditions, and the 45 ci 741, with a low-compression version of the Scout engine. There was very little novelty in these designs, which were heavy – over 450 lb – but virtually indestructible. A much more interesting transverse V-twin with shaft drive was produced at the Army's request and then abandoned, after only a thousand units had been built, when the Jeep was adopted as the standard Army vehicle – much easier to drive, as well as carrying four (or more) people. A major problem for Indian was that they had sold so many of their machine tools that, quite simply, they were unequipped to meet the sudden demand. To be sure, 42,000-odd machines were supplied to the Allies, but this was really a matter of pure luck on Indian's part. The end of hostilities in 1945 left Indian distinctly embarrassed, with a far greater parts inventory than was warranted and for which, furthermore, Uncle Sam refused to pay. Later in that year came the now inevitable re-reorganisation, this time with Ralph Rogers buying out the company. His intention was to produce modern English-style single-cylinder and parallel-twin motorcycles, but he had reckoned without the determined commitment to the big V-twin of American motorcyclists in general, and American dealers in particular. In 1946 production of the old Chief was temporarily re-started, and such was the response that Rogers had to tell everyone that Scouts would also be reintroduced as soon as production of the new machines was under way. The 13 ci (213cc) single and 26 ci (426cc) parallel twin were apparently too fragile for the average ham-fisted American rider who was used to big V-twins built like tractors and, in order to buy time, yet another financial operation was undertaken, with the British Brockhouse Company coming in for $1.5 million (£395,000 at the then exchange rate). This was the kiss of death for Indian, because neither Brockhouse nor Rogers seem to have had much idea of how to exploit the

Indian Brave, 1939.

Indian name. The best that can be said of them is probably that they were ahead of their time, as witness the tremendous growth in lightweight motorcycles since 1965, which both of them predicted. Internal politicking led to the resignation of Rogers – who went on to make good in other fields, as he had already made good before – and the Indian Motorcycle Company was carved into separate manufacturing and sales companies, but by 1953 the whole operation had pretty much ground to a halt. A small batch of Indian Chiefs was built for the New York Police Department in 1955, allegedly as a result of some very dubious specification-rigging, but the mighty Indian company, once one of the greatest names in the whole motorcycling world, effectively ceased to make V-twins in the early 1950s; a sad end.

Although at one time Harley-Davidson, Indian and Excelsior were known as the Big Three American motorcycle manufacturers, there was never much doubt that Excelsior ran a clear third except, perhaps, for a brief while in competition in the 'teens of this century. I hope, therefore, that Excelsior fans will forgive me if I devote the last paragraph of this chapter not to the

Chicago machine but to a much rarer American superbike, one around which legends have grown up, the Crocker.

The Crocker is bound to be mentioned wherever knowledgeable enthusiasts of American motorcycles gather, but what is said will vary because so little is known about it. Between 1936 and 1941 total production was probably just over a hundred. The machine was heavily influenced by Indian practice, but the 45° ohv V-twin was of their own manufacture (as the angle indicates), and at the standard 61 ci displacement it was close to square in bore and stroke. The massively thick cylinder walls allowed considerable overboring, and it was apparently possible to bore it out to an oversquare engine displacing up to 90 ci (1474cc). Primary drive was by quadruplex chain, and final drive from the 3-speed gearbox by conventional chain. The frame was also entirely of Crocker's own design, so the old rumours about the machine being built from a mixture of Harley and Indian components are quite untrue although, inevitably, some of the proprietary components were common to all three makes. The whole design made extensive use of cast aluminium, including even the fuel tank halves, and the whole machine was unbelievably costly to produce. Albert Crocker is reputed to have lost $2,500 on each and every machine produced. There is extraordinarily little information on the Crocker anywhere, the most useful probably being Harry Sucher's excellent appendix to *The Iron Redskin*, his definitive history of Indian motorcycles.

4
Across the Pond

Before World War One the evolution of the big V-twin followed much the same course in both Europe and America, with America (and especially Indian) making the running as often as not. But there were differences, and as the century progressed they became more and more evident.

The first and most obvious difference was the vastly greater number of manufacturers in Europe. This was a result of four things. One, Europe was (and is) a collection of nation-states, each pursuing its own interests and selling in its own market, often with tariff barriers to prevent competition from neighbouring nation-states, although, as we shall see, there was a surprising degree of international trade, especially in proprietary engines. Two, Europe contained the most industrialised country in the world – Great Britain – and many of the other countries were then also far more industrialised than the United States, which was still very rural. Three, the greater population density in Europe meant that it was possible for a small manufacturer to make a good living in his own area, without really trying to sell his goods any further afield. Four, the diversity and variety of industrialisation encouraged the growth of manufacturers who were really only assemblers, firms who took an engine from here and wheels from there and a gear box from somewhere else, and assembled the whole package into their own frame, which might itself be made for them by another sub-contractor.

The second major difference lay in the roads themselves, and in the places they served. European roads were, for the most part, much twistier but vastly better surfaced than those in America (though they were still very rough and crude by modern standards). As a result, there was not the same demand for a big, rugged machine which could plough through mud or across rutted dirt, but there was a need for manoeuvrability and handling. The towns and villages were much closer together, so there was not the need for the effortless long-term power delivery of a big motor; and in the towns and villages streets were much narrower and more crowded, so smaller, lighter machines were at a premium. It is also worth remembering that the price of any machine is surprisingly closely related to its weight, which provided another incentive to European manufacturers to build lighter motorcycles, an option which was not really open to the Americans, who needed brute strength.

The third major difference was closely related to the degree of industrialisation of Europe and America, and to the mechanical sophistication of motorcycle buyers. In Europe there were, relatively, many more skilled mechanics. This allowed more complex engine designs, even if it entailed more maintenance; and most European customers were rather more aware of the need for maintenance, so bikes for the European market did not need to to quite so 'idiot-proof' as those for America.

If people doubt that these distinctions still hold surprisingly good, even though the United States has become far more industrialised and the surface of most American roads is now at least equal to the best in Europe, let them try to ride from (say) Los Angeles to Las Vegas on a 250cc motorcycle or, alternatively, to ride from Exeter to Cambridge via London on a Honda Goldwing or a full-dress Harley.

There was also a fourth difference. The *big* V-twin followed much the same evolutionary path in Europe and America until World War One, but there was also a tradition in Europe of smaller V-twins, where the twin-cylinder layout was used more to provide flexibility and smooth power delivery than sheer power *per se*. For example, Royal Enfield made a 346cc V-twin motorcycle with an MAG engine before 1914, and from 1904 Moto-Reve had built V-twins with capacities as small as 274cc (used in the 1907 Energette), 298cc, 403cc and 497cc. After the war, Peugeot made 295cc and 344cc V-twins as well as 738cc and 746cc models, and many manfacturers made V-twins of 500cc (or thereabouts), despite the fact that others were making singles of 600cc, 700cc and even 800cc. In the United States, of course, 45 cubic inches (750cc) was regarded as a boy's bike (much as 350cc

Ariel – MAG, 1924. This machine has lived in the same square mile of Birmingham since it was first bought.

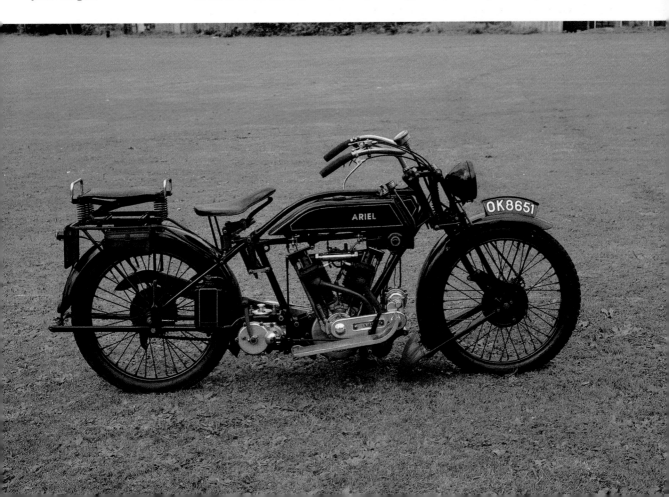

used to be in England), and the minimum size for a 'real' motorcycle was 61 cubic inches, 1000cc, while 74 ci (1200cc) or even 80 ci (1340cc) displacements were not out of the way. It is true that there were a few 1150cc bikes in Europe, and the Bismarck (1904–8) was a 1300cc giant, but for the most part 1000cc was the limit, and even 750cc was a big motorcycle. Of course, there were always the record-breakers and racers from JAP, Peugeot, Anzani and others, with capacities in the early years of as much as 2700cc, but they were scarcely a part of the mainstream of motorcycle design.

It was not until after World War One, though, that the differences between the big European V-twins and the big American V-twins became really marked. To begin with – although many small firms disappeared as a

The V-twin engine Royal Enfield – in a variety of capacities up to 1100cc – was to be found hauling big chairs for decades. This is a 1921 flat-tank model.

result of the war, and the number of suppliers of proprietary engines began to dwindle – there were still many more manufacturers in Europe than remained in the United States. And although manufacturers who could do everything themselves began to gain the upper hand, there was still a firm place for the manufacturer of specialised sports motorcycles, usually with proprietary engines. In the United States, as we have seen, motorcycle design stagnated in the face of competition from the car manufacturers, but this was not to happen in Europe for many years. Instead, as specific power outputs rose, and it became possible to extract as much power from a 500cc single as from a pre-war 1000cc twin, the big twin began to polarise into two different forms.

The first was the soft-tuned side-valve 'slogger', designed to pull a heavy sidecar for the family man or the tradesman. Not until the 1950s did the motor-car begin to compete with the motorcycle and sidecar for initial low cost and economy of running, and even as late as the 1960s I can remember seeing window-cleaners with box sidecars to carry their ladders, though by that time they were not using V-twins! The Royal Automobile Club and the Automobile Association also used to equip their patrolmen with outfits, the coffin-like sidecar containing their tools and equipment. In those days, it was still the custom for a patrolman to salute whenever he saw a member's car

Shallow curves remind us that panel-beating was too expensive an art to be lavished on cheap transport.

A beautifully cast RE magneto drive-chain cover.

displaying the badge; if he did not salute, the member was supposed to stop and ask why. The story was that this was so that the members could be given warning of police speed-traps . . .

The classic 'slogger' was probably the 770cc side-valve from BSA, the company's first V-twin, introduced in 1921. It was joined by a 986cc version in 1922, and these two machines were typical of a whole generation of motorcycles. Similar machines using the manufacturers' own engines came from AJS (990cc and 550cc), Clyno (925cc), Husqvarna (992cc and 546cc) and Royal Enfield (996cc), while many others used proprietary engines: Aza

(Czechoslovakia, JAP engine), New Imperial (JAP until 1926, when they introduced their own engines), Standard (MAG), and many others. Engine suppliers included not only JA Prestwich of Tottenham (JAP) and *Motosacoche à Geneve* (MAG), but also Anzani, and Barr and Stroud, though Fafnir had succumbed to the war and Moto Reve never really recovered from it.

The second stream – the one with which we are much more concerned here – was the 'super sports' machine. Many of the so-called 'sports' V-twins of the 1920s – and 1930s too, for that matter – were nothing more than slightly warmed-up versions of the standard side-valve machines, with 'fir-cone' valve caps which only slightly improved cooling but added considerably to the sporting appearance of the engines to which they were fitted. It is important to remember, though, that the vast majority of the motor-cars of the period were quite unbelievably gutless, and that even a modest motorcycle possessed acceleration and a top speed which put it in the same class as all but the very fastest cars of the time.

The AJS twins of the 1920s were built more for power than for speed.

There were, however, other machines which were undoubtedly the forerunners of modern superbikes. The Brough Superior has a chapter all to itself, but it was not the only machine of its kind nor yet the fastest. Its success was probably due in equal parts to its all-round excellence (speed, handling, finish, detail and comfort) and to its maker's flair for publicity. Two others which were, if anything, even more vivid were the McEvoy-Anzani and the Krammer-Anzani.

In the days when Indian motorcycles had led the world, both they and Harley-Davidson had experimented with 4-valve heads for racing, but had drawn the line at fitting them to road-going machines. In Britain the

Opposite below:
Zenith-Jap. Even in the
early 1930s, assembled
motorcycles with an engine
from JAP, a gearbox from
Burman, and Miller or
Lucas electrics were still
common.

Below:
Probably just after World
War One: Royal Enfield at
their peak. Note the factory
outfits in the background.

proprietary engine firm of Anzani also built an 8-valve V-twin, and this was fitted both to the British McEvoy and the Austrian Krammer in the mid-to-late 1920s. At a time when overhead valves were still regarded as rather special (there were several side-valve models even of the Brough Superior), 4-valve heads were really something. The McEvoy-Anzani in particular was one of the fastest machines on the road in its time, especially after (as was usually the case) the engine had been 'breathed on'. Both of these Super Sports bikes lasted for less than half a decade, but they deserve to be better remembered than they are.

Even in the 1920s, there was still room for experiment, and some of the more unusual (not to say eccentric) designs included two-stroke V-twins from Stanger (538cc, 1921–1923), WAG (496cc, 1924–1925), and Ercoli-Cavallone (496cc, 1922–1923); the Barr and Stroud sleeve-valve engine, which was admirably quiet, but drank oil and proved to have no significant advantages over the poppet-valve (it appeared in the 996cc Grindlay-Peerless in 1923, as well as in the occasional Brough Superior); and a

transverse 246cc engine for the 1926 Phelon and Moore Panthette. But although the 1920s are regarded by many as the golden age of motorcycle manufacture, the technical improvements were probably not as significant as those of the 1930s. To be sure, most manufacturers adopted the saddle tank, which made their machines look much more modern, and all-chain drive replaced belts. Throttle control, however, was still by lawnmower lever in most cases and rear ends were mostly rigid (riders' as well as machines' after a long ride!); valve gear clattered about in the open, total-loss lubrication (albeit by engine-driven pump) was the norm, and the gear shift was still commonly to be found on the side of the tank. Certainly there were improvements in carburettors, in breathing and in metallurgy, but these were slow and steady. The oft-despised 1930s were to see much more dramatic changes.

It is undeniably true that the depression hit many people, and hit them

63

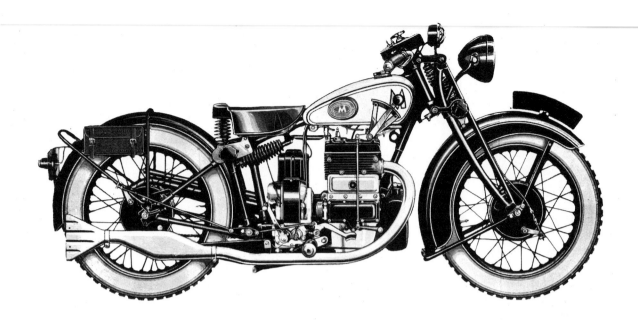

Above:
The Matchless Silver Arrow, a very unconventional (26°) V-twin.

Opposite above:
Zenith – JAP, with 'fir-cone' valve cooling caps – a common feature on sporting side-valves in the 1920s.

Right:
A cutaway of the Silver Arrow engine.

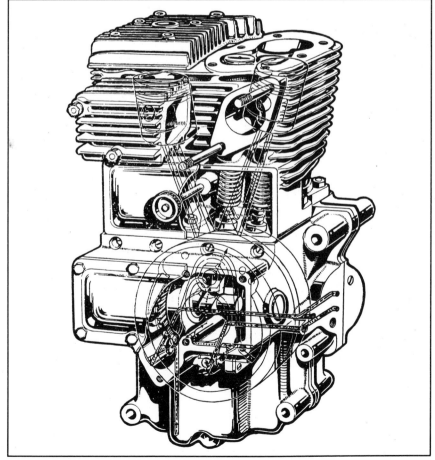

Opposite:
Cast alloy was extensively used on this Ariel-MAG. Note also the external hold-down bars for the cylinders.

hard. It caused the demise of many motorcycle manufacturers who had not modernised sufficiently in the 1930s, or whose marketing base was too small to allow them to survive a recession. But it also redirected the public's attention to motorcycles, at least in Europe. In the United States, the cheap car had captured many erstwhile motorcyclists and would-be motorcyclists for good, and for those who could not afford a new car there were plenty to be had second-hand. In Europe, though, the cheap car had not yet established itself when the depression came, and for many who wanted powered personal transport it was a motorcycle or nothing.

An immediate effect of the depression was to call into being all sorts of very small, very cheap machines – often two-strokes, almost invariably singles – as a way of keeping the motorcycle factories going. But in parallel with this the hard-pressed manufacturers also tried to reflect some glory onto their more boring bread-and-butter machines with flagships, and by racing. The Matchless Silver Arrow was a show-stopper from one of the bigger manufacturers, a 26° side-valve V-twin of 400cc, with the cylinders cast as one monobloc and the heads as another. It was predictably somewhat sluggish and cooling was not all it might have been, but it did look impressive! The leader in show-stoppers was of course George Brough, but it is interesting that he hardly ever used V-twins for this purpose. His specially-made in-line four, the Austin-engined twin-rear-wheel bike for sidecars, and the Golden Dream are far better remembered.

Despite the hard times, technical advances did come fairly thick and fast. The smaller 500cc V-twins grew overhead valves in 1929–31 (the big side-valves simply got bigger), and twist-grip throttles began to be accepted on all but the cheapest machines, where levers lingered until World War Two. (I once owned a 1939 Excelsior Autocycle with a lawnmower-type throttle control.) The positive-stop foot change, pioneered by Velocette in 1928, was rapidly adopted by most other manufacturers, though many offered an auxiliary hand lever for those who did not trust such new-fangled innovations. Dry-sump lubrication became almost universal, and pistons acquired scraper rings, which increased the interval between decarbonising by a factor of five or ten; in the 1920s and early 1930s, it was by no means unusual to have to decoke the engine every 1000–1500 miles.

The V-twin was, however, with very few exceptions no longer in the forefront of technical innovation. Instead, attention was concentrated primarily on the single. This simple engine was cheaper to make, an important consideration in a depression, and it was possible to get 100 mph performance out of a 500cc single. For sidecar pullers, the 'Big Pussy' singles from Panther offered adequate torque and power from a much simpler and cheaper engine than a V-twin. Racing concentrated on the single, with some extraordinarily efficient designs such as the 'double-knocker' overhead cam Nortons and the four-valve Rudges. The only advances in V-twins were made for the out-and-out Super Sports machines, such as the Brough and the Vincent, which both have chapters to themselves.

There was a steady market in the form of government agencies, it was true, and firms such as René-Gillet in France, or Universal in Switzerland, survived almost entirely on this business. Government spending was increasing all over Europe throughout the 1930s, as more and more countries began to realise that National Socialism could lead only to war. When the war came, it changed the face of European motorcycling.

Many firms were simply wiped out, physically or economically. Others went over to war work and never returned to motorcycles after the war. Yet others fell victim to the Russians, who in some cases proved little better than the Nazis whom they replaced. The Czech motorcycle industry, for example, which had been a centre of innovation even before the country gained its independence from the Austro-Hungarian Empire in 1919, was relegated to a backwater. (As an aside, one of the most interesting side-effects of researching this book was to realise just how important Czechoslovakia had been in the history of motorcycling, combined with a sneaking suspicion that some Czech motorcycles – notably the 598cc Bohmerland singles – were a unique expression of the Czech sense of humour.)

After the war, German firms were forbidden to produce big motorcycles,

Once upon a time BSA were famous for V-twins, not parallel ones.

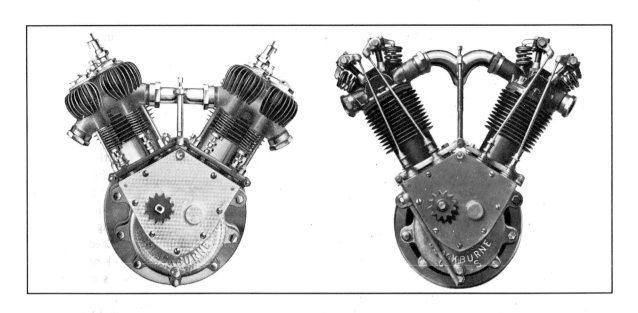

and even if they had made them there would have been few buyers: the war had impoverished everyone. The French could have made bigger machines and, indeed, did make a few René-Gillets, and the like, for the government, as well as a 350cc Motobecane, but the market overall was austere and economy-minded to an extent that it had never been in the 1930s. The Russians, who had made a few Harley-Davidson clones in the 1930s and during the war, switched to mock-BMWs using captured plans (they overran the BMW works at Eisenach, and had access to information from other plants), and stifled almost all technical advance in the countries they invaded; in any case, big V-twins smacked too much of indulgence and people enjoying themselves, which went against the spirit of Marxism-Leninism. Only Vincent remained to fly the flag of the V-twin sports bike in Europe, and when Vincent went under in 1955 it looked as if only Harley-Davidson would keep the faith, but times were to change as we shall see. Meanwhile, we shall look at two of the more unusual aspects of the V-twin: the flat twin, which is effectively a 180° V-twin, and the V-twin 3-wheeler.

5
The 180° Twin

Long before the Bayerische Flugzeugwerke considered making motorcycles, a Bristolian called Joseph Barter designed a flat-twin motorcycle which he called the Fée or Fairy. Opposed-piston or 'boxer' engines were not new – it is said that Barter himself was inspired by Lanchester's flat six – but when Walter Moore put one of Barter's engines into a motorcycle in 1905, he laid the foundations of a classic design. The original 200cc engine was designed so that both cylinders fired simultaneously, which led to widely spaced delivery of the power strokes and placed quite a strain on the bottom end, but the production version used a more conventional 180° firing interval. It seems that the con-rods were offset from the very start, rather than being of the 'knife and fork' variety.

Although the Fée was not a great success, the design (and designer) were taken over by Douglas Brothers, also of Bristol, and the famous 'Douggie' was born. The capacity rose to 340cc, 2¾ fiscal horsepower, and in 1910 a two-speed gearbox was added. The next major improvement was the adoption of mechanically operated inlet valves. A 663cc prototype engine was built in 1911, and in 1912 this arrangement replaced automatic inlet valves on production models. In the 1912 Junior TT, Douglases finished first, second and fourth. A slight increase in bore (to 61mm) gave a swept volume of 349cc for the 1913 models, and in 1914 a new 3½ hp model appeared, to be joined in 1915 by a 600cc 4 hp model with a three-speed gearbox, designed mainly for sidecar use. This was not the biggest engine which the firm had built to date, because the 1911 prototype had been expanded still further to 965cc (85 × 85 mm) for 1912, but it had appeared in a Williamson, a vanishingly rare make which it has been suggested was actually only a Douglas built under another name, because of family disputes about the value of having a really big machine in the line-up.

During World War One production concentrated on the smaller models, and the Douggie became one of the two standard army DR (despatch rider) bikes, the other being the Model H Triumph. Apart from occasional trouble with shorting of the front plug, caused by water splashes, the Douggies gave sterling service at the front, and by 1918 the Army had bought about 25,000 of the Bristol-built bikes.

The first really new models appeared in 1921, with new 494cc and 733cc overhead-valve engines. The smaller version was 'square' at 68 × 68 mm, and the extra capacity was obtained by boring the smaller engine to 83 mm, an unusually oversquare design for the period. Both featured all-chain drive and a 3-speed gearbox, though the chain-primary/belt-secondary drive was

Douggies made a great name on the dirt tracks of the 1920s. The chrome bar strapped to the tank and frame is a leg support to aid broadsiding (and leg-breaking!)

even in the 1920s, for at a time when some of the older firms were already giving up on the idea, William Brough, father of George Brough, made his last flat twin (and his last motorcycle) in 1923, the same year that Humber gave up on the configuration. The Czech Itar appeared in 1921 and lasted until 1929, and the German Hochland had an even shorter life, from about 1926 to 1927. The Wooler (always a limited-production *marque*) appeared in 346cc and 496cc guises all through the 1920s and well into the 1930s. Harley-Davidson tried the in-line flat-twin concept in the early 1920s, and found it wanting (Indian had already tried and rejected it in 1917, with their 'mock Douglas'), but Mars in Germany powered one of their most successful motorcycles with a 956cc engine built especially for them by Maybach, who also made the engines for Zeppelins. The famous 'White Mars' ran from 1920 to the 1930s, though production stopped for about eighteen months at the height of the Weimar inflation in 1924–1926.

Apart from Douglas, there were really only two successful makers of in-line flat twins after 1930, namely Victoria in Germany and Coventry-Victor in England. The original Victoria of 1922 had been powered by the 500cc 6½ hp (fiscal) BMW-made engine, but when BMW started making their own motorcycles this source dried up, and Victoria brought out their own

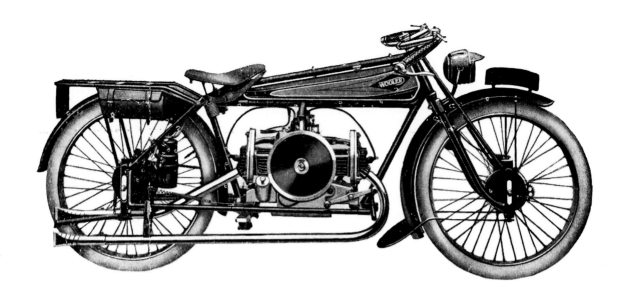

A high centre of gravity is not easy to achieve with a flat-twin, but both Humber (1914) and Wooler (1929) managed it.

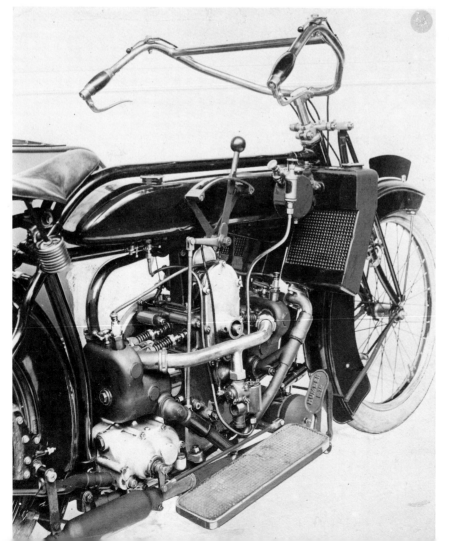

overhead valve 500cc and 600cc engines. They even supercharged them in 1925, and enjoyed some success in racing. The *marque* improved slowly but steadily for a while, but then stagnated in the 1930s, and the last in-line twins were produced either in the late 1930s or in the early years of the war. Coventry-Victor produced flat twins in a variety of sizes, from 500cc to 750cc, between 1919 and 1936. As well as powering the makers' own machines, these engines also appeared in the vanishingly rare McKechnie of the early 1920s, and in various European motorcycles such as the Bison (Austria) and the Jeecy-Vea (Belgium).

In the end it was probably the poor cooling of the rear cylinder, the vulnerability of the front sparking plug to water-induced shorting, and the long wheelbase of the in-line flat twin which led to its demise. In side-valve days engine length was, of course, less and because power outputs were lower, heat dissipation was less of a problem; but it is worth noting that no really new flat twins were introduced after the beginning of the 1930s. Unlike the V-twin, where the in-line layout was to prove much more successful than transverse mounting, it was the transverse flat twin which was to have the upper hand, as we shall see in Chapter 8. Of course, there is always the possibility that Honda may revive the layout, perhaps with water cooling, for a 250cc engine: just look at their VT250 . . .

6
The 3-Wheeled V-Twin

Cyclecars, those curious hybrids between motor-cars and motorcycles, have a history as long as that of powered transport. Mostly they were conceived as a cheap and somewhat basic means of transport for two people (though there have been four-seater family models and single-seater racers), and have been distinctly nasty. But there is one which cannot be ignored in any book about V-twins, and another which deserves inclusion because of its sheer impudence, and because it is a vehicle out of its time. The first is, of course, the Morgan and the second is the Tri-King.

Henry Frederick Stanley Morgan, or HFS as he was normally known, built a minimalist single-seater with tiller steering in the first decade of the century. It was a simple, not to say crude, design. A 4-hp single or 8-hp V-twin JAP engine sat at the front of a tubular spine chassis, with a cross-member to the two front wheels, and a prop-shaft ran from the clutch at the engine end to a bevel box under the seat, where a two-speed 'gearbox' was created by the simple expedient of engaging either of two chain-wheels by means of a dog clutch controlled by a lever. The lower engine bearing tubes

The wiper is a contemporary accessory, and you can see the hand throttle on the lower left.

JAP and Matchless provided the engines for most Morgans.

acted as exhaust pipes, and a negligible amount of bodywork provided some protection from mud and dirt.

Although an appearance at the Motor Cycle Show at Olympia in 1910 did not produce the kind of response Morgan had been hoping for, he decided to persevere and to advertise his vehicle in the best way possible, in competition. Although the Morgan was conceived as a utility runabout (and was always described on the dash plate as the Morgan Runabout), it is important to remember that *any* mechanically-powered vehicle in those days was regarded primarily as a means of sport rather than of transport, so even the most unlikely vehicles sought a sporting image in competitions, trials and hill-climbs. These events also performed a very useful function, in that they winnowed the wheat from the chaff in the full glare of publicity, so that the real mechanical disasters quickly became known while the designs with potential or actual merit could be demonstrated to all and sundry.

The London to Exeter trial at the very end of 1910 saw HFS winning a

Morgan Sports model, 1933.

gold medal, and in May 1911 he was awarded a certificate in the Auto-Cycle Union quarterly trials. Another gold followed in the London to Edinburgh trial in the following month, and the general consensus was that the Morgan was definitely beginning to prove itself.

The design of these winning cyclecars was still very primitive, apart from the Morgan sliding-pillar front suspension (still used to this day), but in August 1911 several decisive changes were made. Two-seater bodywork was fitted, and the vehicle acquired a car-type steering wheel. As a design both sporting and practical it was very promising, and when HFS exhibited again at the 1911 Motor Cycle Show there was no longer a shortage of interest.

In March 1912, a 2-seater Morgan with a '90 bore' (90 × 77.5 mm, 986cc) JAP engine won a scratch race organised at Brooklands by the British Motor Cycle Racing Club. It won by a lead of two minutes, which is impressive in any race, but staggering in a race which was over (at least so far as first place was concerned!) in eight minutes and thirty two seconds. This was the real turning point in Morgan's fortunes. Over a hundred orders were apparently received as a direct result of this race.

78

Fifty years on: the Tri-King, 1983.

Thereafter, the Morgan changed astonishingly little in concept, though the engines steadily became more and more powerful. Although JAP made the engines which are always associated with the Morgan in most people's minds, various types (OHV and SV) were fitted, and throughout the life of the three-wheeler there were others. Water cooling was tried in 1913, with the now forgotten Blumfield engine, and capacities varied from an air-cooled 670cc Blumfield (for the 750cc class) to the usual one-litre versions by JAP, Precision and others: There were also models which displaced more than a litre, such as the 1093cc MAG and the 1129cc Quadrant. There were water-cooled JAPs, as well as air-cooled, and as early as 1913 a curious four-speed arrangement was being tried, with a two-speed 'cascade' box just behind the clutch. The effect was similar to the transfer box on a Land-Rover, in that it multiplied the two-speed final drive by two, to give four speeds.

At various times the chassis was lengthened and widened – which improved stability – and it was 'beefed up' repeatedly, but over the years the power of the engines fitted to the racing versions rose to over 100 bhp, at

If you drive a Tri-King in the rain, you lean out and wear goggles – and this is what you see!

Racing Morgans is a fine tradition, as this shot taken in April 1914 shows.

which point the rear wheel was inclined to wander all over the place, twisting and wobbling furiously. This was a problem which could not be solved by mere beefing up, and although fitting shock absorbers (not standard equipment) improved matters considerably, a late Morgan can be altogether excessively exciting to drive!

The first really major change to the design came in 1930, when a 'three-speed plus reverse' gearbox was fitted in place of the old bevel box, and in 1933 Matchlesses replaced JAPs as the standard engine, though all sorts of 'go-faster' specials were still made quite regularly. Thereafter, changes were once more a matter of detail only right up to the demise of the V-twin Morgan, after World War Two. The demise was occasioned not so much by the lack of V-twin engines, as is often said, as by the 'export or die' policies of the then British government (3-wheelers were not particularly exportable) and by the increasing cost of manufacture, which made the price differential between three-wheelers and four-wheelers ever smaller. The last 3-wheeler (albeit with a Ford engine, rather than a V-twin) was actually made in 1952, just over half a century after HFS Morgan had founded his claim to immortality in the annals of motor sport, three-wheelers and V-twins.

There is, however, an interesting postscript to the history of the Morgan. In 1977, long-time Morgan owner Tony Divey decided to build a light, fast, manoeuvrable V-twin runabout based on the Moto-Guzzi transverse V-twin, and he succeeded with a vengeance. The Tri-King, as he called his creation, attracted so much interest that he decided to go into limited production in 1978, and his is a remarkable vehicle. The big Moto-Guzzi engine (in various capacities) and five-speed gearbox are used in their entirety, and the Moto-Guzzi swinging arm/hub/wheel assembly at the back provides far more positive location of the rear wheel than the chain-drive Moggies ever managed. The front end features a delightful double-wishbone front suspension which is (dare one say it) vastly superior to the old Morgan, and the handling (once you are used to the power and the very short wheelbase) is excellent.

The positive-stop gear shift mechanism is perhaps a bit of a problem, though more so for car drivers than for motorcyclists, and with a power-to-weight ratio of around 200 bhp/ton even before you start tuning or playing with 4-valve heads, etc, the little beastie is very quick indeed. The top speed is comfortably in excess of 100 mph (though handling is a bit skittish as you approach the three-figure mark), and the Tri-King recaptures the magic of Morgan three-wheelers and adds a good bit of its own, even if the price is close to 90% of that of a Moggie four-wheeler.

7
Guaranteed in Writing

'Every SS100 will be despatched with a written guarantee, signed by the Maker, that the machine has actually been timed over 100 mph for a quarter of a mile.'

Nowadays, 100 mph may not seem all that remarkable but in 1925, when this statement appeared in the Brough Superior catalogue, it was sensational. It is extremely difficult to sort the truth about Brough Superiors from all the myths and the ballyhoo. On the one hand, there are those who say that the Brough Superior was the greatest motorcycle of all time, and that George Brough could do no wrong, and on the other, there are those who point out that he never made his own engines or gearboxes, that most of the other components were also bought in, and that Broughs were merely another assembled motorcycle, distinguished chiefly by their maker's talent for marketing and publicity.

As ever, the truth lies somewhere between the two but, in all fairness, it does seem that there is more truth in the praise than in the condemnation. There is no doubt that George Brough was a consummate showman, and never missed a chance for publicity. For example, there is the famous story about Rolls Royce management being somewhat worried about the way in which the Brough Superior was known as 'the Rolls Royce of motorcycles', and sending along a couple of inspectors. The gentlemen from Derby were shown into the paint shop, where men in white gloves were fussing over an immaculately finished petrol tank. Well satisfied that Rolls Royce standards were, indeed, observed at Brough's , the Rolls men left, without discovering that the tank in question was destined for a show model and that ordinary customers' machines did not receive quite the same attention. On the other hand, there is no other serious contestant for the title of 'the Rolls Royce of motorcycles' throughout the entire life of the Brough, if you take 'Rolls Royce' to mean the smoothest, best finished, most excellently detailed and most elegant, with considerably better than average performance. In fact, it is arguable that only one other manufacturer has ever aimed at the same market as the Brough Superior – the Hesketh, which is covered in Chapter 11.

George Brough's father, WE Brough, was also a motorcycle manufacturer, though he seems only to have made one V-twin, in 1911. He was a devotee of the fore-and-aft flat twin, which he continued to manufacture until 1923. Just after World War One, his son mooted the idea of making a super-luxury high-performance motorcycle, but WE Brough was not convinced, so George set up on his own, on perfectly amicable terms (contrary to some reports).

Brough SS80, 1920s.

The first Brough Superior appeared in late 1919. Unlike his father, George used bought-in engines, and his first machine began the tradition of using JAP engines. It was a 50° ohv V-twin, of 90 mm bore and 77.5 mm stroke, giving a total swept volume of 986cc. The pistons were of light alloy, with two compression rings and a scraper ring, and lubrication (on a total-loss basis) was controlled by a hand plunger or foot pump, both being fitted to all machines. The gearbox was a three-speed Sturmey-Archer, and one of the most striking visual features of the machine was the saddle tank – apparently the first of its kind. Both the JAP engine and the Sturmey-Archer box were specially made for George Brough, and there is little doubt that they were of the best quality which their makers could attain, even if they were not quite as exclusive and novel in all their features as Brough liked to pretend. On this point, it is worth remembering that in those comparatively low-tech days, with cheap and highly skilled labour, it was a good deal easier to have engines, etc, customised to suit a particular buyer's requirements, so the often-made gibe that Broughs were 'only' assembled machines betrays a certain ignorance of the way in which things used to be done. Besides, the degree of sub-contracting that goes on nowadays is hardly ever realised by those outside the trade.

There was also a side-valve version of the same machine, with an 85.5 × 85 mm (988cc) JAP engine, and the so-called Mk II, which was powered by a

748 cc (72 × 90 mm) MAG ioe engine. Shortly afterwards, there was also a Brough Superior powered by a 999cc (86 × 86 mm square) 50° Barr and Stroud engine, with sleeve valves, a rare machine – even by Brough standards – but one which shows that George was of an experimental turn of mind, and that his show-stopping exhibition models were not just showmanship, as has so often been said.

The first machines were very well received, though once again it is difficult to determine just how good they were, because the road-testers of the day were habitually so lavish in their praise of even truly awful machines that they had no new words to use when they were faced with a really excellent motorcycle. Encouraged by success, George brought out a whole new machine in 1924, the SS80. Based once again on the 988cc side-valve JAP design, the new engine used two cams instead of one and twin valve-springs, and the motorcycle which it powered was capable of 80 mph.

The SS designation was to be made far more famous by his next machine, the SS100. This immortal machine was designed in 1923-4, and first offered for sale for the 1925 season (that is, late in 1924). With an almost square 85.5 × 86 mm engine (980cc), it was a development of the old '90 bore' with lightened valve gear, and lubrication was by mechanical pump, though still total-loss. A figure of 1450 mpg oil consumption was claimed, and fuel consumption could range from around 50 mpg when driven really hard, to 70 mpg or more when driven more normally. This was the machine which was guaranteed, in writing, to 100 mph.

If you get a chance to handle one of these old machines nowadays, several features will strike you immediately. The first is how extraordinarily light they are, compared with modern motorcycles of the same displacement. This lightness was one of the things which made them so fast for their power output though, to be fair, it was also made possible by the comparatively low bhp/litre figures of those days. The second is the lack of suspension at the back end, and the distinctly limited travel of the front suspension. 'Hard tails' may be acceptable on modern smooth roads, but on the pot-holed and bumpy roads of the 1920s, they must have been purgatory. Incidentally, the Castle fork used on Broughs was a proprietary unit, but also one which was designed by George Brough and Harold Karslake, so it can hardly be called 'bought in'. The third point is the astonishing lack of brakes on machines which could travel at three-figure speeds. To be sure, there was far less traffic in those days, but anyone who has ridden in (say) India, or even Ireland, can testify that low traffic densities and low speeds simply promote carelessness and unpredictability. Rounding a bend at speed, only to discover a farm cart on the wrong side of the road, requires dramatic braking!

For the 1926 season, the Alpine GS was introduced – a still more 'hotted up' SS100, with triple valve springs on its 80 × 99 mm (988 cc) JAP engine – along with the Pendine, guaranteed in writing to have been tested at 110 mph. The name came, of course, from Pendine sands. In those days the Bonneville salt flats had not yet come into their own for speed attempts, and

Tommy-bars on oil and petrol caps were a feature to make your mouth water in the showroom and your eyes water in a crash stop!

more local venues were used, of which Pendine sands was one of the most famous.

For 1926, a smaller Brough was introduced for the first time, the Overhead 680. With 70 mm bore and 88 mm stroke, the 674 cc ohv engine delivered 25 bhp, which could propel the bike at well over 80 mph. It was sufficiently well received that a side-valve version was offered in 1927 (a 680cc side-valve engine had been in JAP's catalogue for some time), and an economy derivative was also made, the 5–15. Although the sv engine delivered only 17.5 bhp, the sv 680 was still good for 75 mph or so, and could regularly return 80 mpg, though one must remember that the riding styles of those days led to rather better fuel economy than we get nowadays. The 1927 season also saw the SS80 continued, albeit now in two guises. The standard version cost £122.10s.0d, and delivered 25 bhp, but for an extra £7.10s.0d, the De Luxe version had somewhat different valve gear and an extra 5 bhp. There was in addition a side valve 750cc (70 × 97 mm), with comparable performance to the sv 680 but with much softer power delivery.

The overhead 680 was the basis of another legendary Brough, the Black Alpine 680, which was finished in eggshell black and built into a Draper spring frame; one of the better spring frames of the time. It made a delightful middleweight tourer, as well as possessing very striking looks.

The 680 was not, however, the smallest production Brough ever made. That honour belongs to the 500cc version introduced for the 1931 season. Powered by a 62.5 × 80 mm, 498cc JAP motor, it was a curious hybrid, in that it was sold as a tourer which could be easily converted into a racer and back again. By taking off the lights and removing the compression plates under the cylinders, the owner converted a fast but reasonably docile machine into an out-and-out racer. A four-speed gearbox allowed better than 90 mph when running at the racing compression ratio, though in touring trim 85 mph was nearer the mark. Very few of these machines were ever made, and even fewer survive. Indeed most people are unaware that there ever was a Brough Superior of such petite dimensions.

At the other end of the scale, there was the 1096cc (85.7 × 95 mm) side-valve introduced in 1933. It could haul a side-car at up to 75 mph or so and, although it was rarely used in solo form, it could easily exceed 90 mph if it was, and a well set-up version, with tall gearing, could exceed 100 mph, and there were not many side-valve machines capable of that. Unlike the smaller JAP engines this was a 60° vee, so cooling must have been slightly improved and power delivery slightly more even.

There was, however, another machine introduced in late 1933 (for the 1934 season) which eclipsed all other Broughs and is unquestionably one of

Brough OHV 680, c 1926.

Brough SS80, 1937.

the greatest motorcycles of all time. It was the New SS100, with a 996cc (80 × 99 mm) 50° JAP engine delivering no less than 74 bhp – a figure which is more than respectable in the 1980s, and absolutely staggering in the 1930s. With twin carbs, twin magnetos (one a magdyno for lighting), and an 8:1 compression ratio, it was virtually a racing motorcycle in roadgoing trim. It must have been a tremendously exhilarating machine to ride on the virtually deserted roads of the day, even if there were very few places where full power could be unleashed.

From the end of 1935 there was an alternative engine for the SS100, an AMC/Matchless 50° vee with square 85.5 mm bore and stroke, 990cc. Unlike the JAP engine, which used coil valve springs, the AMC engine used the hairpin variety. A lower-rated version of the same engine was also made available for the SS80 at the same time.

AMC also provided the engine for the only transverse-Vee Brough ever made, a side-valve motorcycle introduced in 1937. In keeping with his policy of using bought-in components, George Brough used a modified Austin car box, which was not exactly ideal for motorcycle use, and the transverse Brough is more of a curiosity than a serious Brough Superior. On the other hand, George's proclivities for building improbable motorcycles as showpieces and out of sheer mechanical *joie-de-vivre* is well known; the Austin-engined straight four with two rear wheels laced onto a single hub (for sidecar use only!) was one, the 1927 side-valve V-4 and the 1928 in-line four specially built by MAG are other examples, and the Golden Dream with its

double flat twin is now on show at the British National Motorcycle Museum *Brough SS80.*
near Solihull. This extraordinary machine literally contains two flat twins,
with separate crankshafts geared together, mounted one above the other in a
common crank-case, after the fashion of a Wooler.

The end of the Brough Superior story is a surprisingly sudden one. With
the coming of World War Two, the Brough works went over to manufacturing military *materiel*, and at the war's end motorcycle manufacture was not
resumed. The reason given in most histories is that there were no manufacturers of suitable engines left, but this reason is not quite so clear-cut as it
seems. It is true that the big AMC twins were no longer available, but JAP
were still making their V-twins (which were, admittedly, looking increasingly long in the tooth) and one might have thought that the Vincent unit
had its possibilities (though it may be that this route was explored). What
seems more likely is that almost all the infrastructure which was necessary to
support a small specialist assembler/manufacturer had disappeared. Not just
engines but gearboxes, forks and even such unconsidered parts as saddles

SS 80 Brough Superior Models.

Mark I. Side Valve
Mark I. Overhead
Mark II. Standard
Mark II. Sports

GRACE!   ELEGANCE!!   SPEED!!!

GEORGE BROUGH, Haydn Road, Nottingham.

IMPORTANT.

PRELUDE. IT is now but two years since the " Brough Superior " was introduced for the connoisseur motor cyclist—the man who demands a machine in a class apart from the ordinary article, of which there are so many different makes, but all so very much alike.   The success of the venture is now well known : and if proof of such success were needed it is to be found in the increasing number of copyists of the " Brough Superior."

It has always been a strict policy of the maker to give every possible after-delivery service to " Brough Superior " riders.   Many delightful letters of appreciation from Riders can be seen at Haydn Road, as also can some most remarkable testimonials on the excellent qualities of the machine—letters of appreciation that have been sent spontaneously and unsolicited by Riders of many years' experience and makers of machines.   Quite apart from the Works' service, the maker of the " Brough Superior " has arranged repair and replacement service for his Riders in London, Manchester, Birmingham, Cambridge, Leeds, Edinburgh, Bournemouth, Exeter, and for Competition Riders on Brookland's track.   Australian Riders have also a Depôt in Sydney catering exclusively for their requirements.

The ambitious specification, coupled with the superb finish of the " Brough Superior," necessarily demands a high selling price, but it is part of the maker's policy to ignore this disadvantage in favour of keeping the " Brough Superior " in a position of unassailable pre-eminence.

The successes gained by private owners riding their own " Brough Superiors " in open Competition of all kinds has been freely commented on in the Press.   In no single instance has a specially built " Brough Superior " toed the line in competition, and this fact confirms the maker's claim that, quite apart from obvious superiority in other features, the " Brough Superior " is the fastest fully equipped touring machine on the road—and it does its speed with such great ease and absence of effort.   This latter quality is the one most freely commented on by " Brough Superior " riders.

This Leaflet introduces an entirely new "Brough Superior " named **SS 80** model, undoubtedly the neatest-looking and most luxurious Sporting machine offered to the public.   Each machine is guaranteed by the maker to have *exceeded* **80 miles per hour**.   For an extra charge a Certificate signed by the Brookland's Track Authorities certifying that the completely equipped Machine, *e.g.*, with 3-speed gear, kick starter, clutch, mudguards, 2 stands, carrier, tools, tool bags, etc., has officially *exceeded* **80 miles per hour** for a Kilometre.   The superiority of such a certificate over one which refers only to the engine will be appreciated.   Further, the purchaser of an " SS 80 " model is cordially invited to see his machine put through its test by the maker's competition service on Brookland's Track.   Apart from the special Engine necessary to substantiate the speed guaranteed, there are many modifications and refinements throughout the whole machine which will be appreciated by present " Brough Superior " Riders.

Even before the SS100, the SS80 was also guaranteed in writing.

and handlebars were no longer readily available from proprietary suppliers. It would have been quite possible to manufacture some of these and to sub-contract others, but the shrunken market, the shortage of money in the post-war years, the British government's restrictions on availability of materials, and the sad fact that the Brough works could support itself very much more profitably by manufacturing other things, all conspired together to spell the end of the Rolls Royce of motorcycles.

There are, however, a few loose ends to be tidied up. Towards the end of World War Two, a totally new Brough/Karslake-designed 90° V-twin was actually built, and tested in a complete motorcycle in 1944. The big twin, with the magdyno and the carburettors between the cylinders, was mounted

125 mph speedometers were not a common sight for many decades.

conventionally (symmetrically about the vertical axis), which allowed a low seat height, and surprisingly enough allowed the wheelbase to be kept the same as on the SS100, which is, in all fairness, still pretty long. In place of the knife and fork con-rods of the JAP and AMC engines, the new engine was not only side-by-side, it was actually double-throw: assembled as a built-up bottom end with *three* integral flywheels, the third being between the two con-rods. This introduced a slight rocking couple, but foreshadowed Honda's design by nearly forty years! It may well be that this engine was what persuaded George Brough that the JAP had had its day. Realising that it would not be economically feasible to produce his own engine, he may have refused to settle for second best.

Finally, the fact that Brough production ceased with the war did not mean that Broughs ceased to be a major force in British motorcycling. In 1949, a specially prepared record-breaker attained 162 mph on Pendine sands, and well into the 1950s there was very little to touch the pre-war road-going models for out-and-out speed. In Britain the Brough Superior Owners Club was one of the first one-make clubs, if not the very first. And by the end of the 1950s, Broughs had already become collectors' items. The comparatively limited numbers made, and the fact that few Brough owners ever relinquished their machines once they got them, meant that they appeared less and less in the second-hand columns and, as fewer and fewer people had the chance to ride one, the legend finally began to overrun the facts.

8
The Wrong Way

The advantages and disadvantages of mounting a V-twin transversely are about equally obvious. On the credit side, you get excellent cooling and an admirably short engine from front to rear, allowing a compact wheelbase. On the debit side, you increase frontal area (and hence drag), and you can no longer use a nice, simple chain drive as, at some point, the drive has to be turned through a right angle, from the direction of crankshaft rotation to the direction of wheel rotation. Also, the cylinders are wont to compete for space

Aimed unerringly (if not aesthetically) at the American market; a V65 custom.

The old and the new. An unusual hint of vandalism in this BMW PR shot!

with a rider's knees, and there is no doubt that bits which stick out at the sides are more vulnerable in the event of a spill than those which are protected inside the frame. The old canard about torque reaction turns out to have little foundation in theory, and virtually none in fact. It is true that if you blip the throttle at rest, you can feel the machine twitch in the opposite direction to engine rotation as the machine tries to rotate around the crankshaft, but once the bike starts moving, you would need to miss a gear in the middle of a corner whilst well heeled over on an adverse camber even to notice it, let alone worry about it.

Given this list of drawbacks, it is not surprising that the transversely mounted V-twin or flat-twin has been an unpopular configuration but, even so, there have been more such designs than might be expected. And when you look at the successful ones, it becomes clear that the drawbacks are mostly more apparent than real.

To begin with, although the increase in the frontal area of the naked motorcycle may be considerable, the increase in the total frontal area of machine *plus rider* is not all that great, especially in the light of the competition for space between a rider's legs and the cylinders of most V-twins. Having to take the drive through a right-angle is a veritable advantage with shaft drive, and the majority of successful transverse twins have used this form of final drive. As for vulnerability, the cylinders and rocker (or cam) boxes of transverse twins are usually a lot tougher than the flimsily-cased ends of the average transverse straight four: a new alternator or even a new crankshaft may be called for in the latter case, whereas it is extremely

Opposite and opposite above: The clear advantages of side-valve design in transverse flat twins.

92

unusual for even a BMW (generally regarded as the height of vulnerability) to require any more than a new rocker box, or perhaps a new head if the owner worries about a couple of cosmetically chipped fins. All in all, the only objection which turns out to have real substance is the one about the cylinders and the knees and, even then, if the bike is properly designed you need to have very long legs before there is any real difficulty: my 6 foot 1 inch brother-in-law rides his Moto-Guzzi V7 with no problems!

It is only fair, though, to return to that question of shaft drive. It is a less efficient method of transferring power from the engine to the back wheel, with a percentage efficiency usually in the low 80s rather than the mid 90s, which makes it less attractive than chain drive for sporting machines. On the other hand, it requires far less maintenance than an exposed chain (a properly enclosed oil-bath chain is another matter), and what efficiency it has, it keeps, which makes it more attractive for touring machines. One additional drawback, however, is that the motorcycle designer is unlikely to be able to use a proprietary gearbox. This was a matter of considerable importance in the past, even if it is substantially irrelevant today.

Clement Ader was building transverse V-twins as far back as 1905 (the company went under in 1906!), and there were many others who tried the same path over the years. Spring from Belgium used 500cc, 750cc and 1000cc transverse motors of their own design in the early 1920s, the French Stylson used transverse JAPs, the short-lived Italian Finzi (1923–1925) was a 600cc design, and the Czech Walter 750cc was built mainly for the Czech Army. The smallest of the pre-war transverse V-twins was the 250cc P&M Panther Panthette, in the late 1920s. None of these was particularly successful, though both the Spring and the Walter were built in quite large numbers. The 1931 AJS, on the other hand, appeared in very small numbers indeed. There was a short-lived Indian shaft-drive transverse twin in the early years of World War Two, and after the war there were another three transverse V-twins introduced in the 1950s. The first was the German 350cc Victoria of about 1953, a neat little ohv unit-construction, shaft-drive machine with an amazingly bulky crank-case, which survived for only three years: the second, in the mid-1950s, was the Japanese Lilac, similar in concept to the Victoria but even smaller at 250cc, which may have lasted to the early 1960s: the third was the Lancer, very similar to the Lilac, from the same country, and at about the same time. In fact, it was not until Moto-Guzzi came along with their V-twins in 1967 that the transverse V-twin really began to get anywhere, and we shall return to these later. Meanwhile, the transverse flat twin had enjoyed a much more successful career.

The flat twin – the 180° vee – had, as we have already seen, been a popular design for many years, though it had normally been mounted fore-and-aft. The seminal transverse flat twin is generally regarded as being the ill-fated 398cc ABC of 1919–20. It was not a reliable engine and the chain drive did not help. It is said that the Bayerische Motoren Werke paid close attention to the design, and their 1923 500cc flat twin may well have been influenced by it. Improvements, however, included unit construction, car-type gearbox

BMW are one of the few manufacturers who supply publicity shots of their motorcycles actually being ridden which, after all, is how they are going to be used – R100RS 1983.

and shaft drive. Designated the R32 for some inscrutable reason, the new motorcycle developed 8.5 bhp from its side-valve design, and was to be the progenitor of a line of motorcycles which retained a recognisably similar basic layout for more than 60 years. At the time of writing, the biggest twins (the R100 series) have been discontinued, but the 800cc and smaller versions still look set to continue for years to come.

To follow the entire development of BMW motorcycles for sixty years or more would serve no useful purpose, but it is worth looking at a few of the highlights and eccentricities of the Bavarian twin's career. In 1925 there came an ohv version, the R37, with 16 bhp instead of $8\frac{1}{2}$, and in 1926 the side-valver was uprated to 12 bhp. Bigger engines also followed: 1928 saw the 750cc R62 and R63, though the two new engines were markedly different. The side-valve R62 was a square 78 × 78 mm 745cc engine delivering 18 bhp, while the ohv R63 delivered 24 bhp from a markedly oversquare 83 × 68 mm 735 cc version. In 1929 came the curious looking, but ingeniously engineered Star pressed-steel frame for the sv R11; it was a striking looking machine by anyone's standards, and apparently suffered from no disadvantages save the conservatism of motorcycle buyers.

Throughout the 1930s power outputs rose steadily. The 1935 ohv R17 delivered 33 bhp from 734cc, and its 500cc sister the R5 delivered 24 bhp, though the side-valve units remained much more modest with 18 bhp for

95

both the 745cc R12 (1935) and the 600cc R6 (1937), and the R61 (1938). A foot shift (with supplementary hand lever) was introduced on the R5 in 1936, and the R51 (494cc, ohv) grew rear suspension in 1938. But then the war was upon them, and the race-tracks of Europe no longer resounded to the scream of supercharged racing models, and no more records would fall to Meier and Henne.

BMW supplied many solo motorcycles to the German armed services, mostly 'cooking' side valves, but an interesting aside on German conscription was that motorcyclists were required to bring their BMWs or other German motorcycles with them when they joined up, though they could leave other makes at home! The Germans were also great believers in the side-car, and among the outfits supplied by BMW was one of the most interesting machines ever built, the R75 with sidecar drive. It was a 745cc ohv machine, but with a compression ratio of only 5.6 or 5.8:1, to allow the use of poor fuel and restrict performance in the interests of safety, the latter a curious anomaly in view of its intended use! A power take off just forward of the rear hub centre drove a short transverse prop-shaft which ran under the sidecar chassis at the rear and was geared to the sidecar wheel. With only 26 bhp the R75 outfit was not fast, but a transfer box giving eight forward and two reverse gears, plus a lockable differential, made it virtually unstoppable. It was a tremendous handful to manage, and the sidecar passenger was apparently called upon to assist with gear changing on the tricky bits, but in

'Mulo meccanico' – the Italian Army's mechanical mule, 1960–1963.

96

the hands of a truly fearless pilot it was and is (according to those brave enough to ride in them) one of the ultimate cross-country vehicles. Apart from the weight, which at 880 lb was little more than a modern full-dresser solo Harley-Davidson, the only real drawback was its prodigious appetite for rear tyres.

After the war, BMW's corporate wrist was slapped by the Allies, who prohibited the production of any motorcycles bigger than 250cc. BMW met this restriction by manufacturing what amounted to half of a 500cc twin and turning the lonely pot upright; a formula they had tried as early as 1925 with the 247cc ohv R39, and had explored in various capacities from 198cc to 398cc throughout the pre-war years. But in 1950, the 494cc twins returned, to be joined a year later by the 590cc (72 × 73 mm) R67. These remained the standard BMW capacities until 1969, during which time the power output of the 500s rose from 24 bhp to 35 bhp (R50S), and that of the 600s rose from 26 bhp to 42 bhp (R69S). It was undeniable, though, that the BMW design was looking increasingly long in the tooth and that price differentials between BMWs and other machines were so high that mostly it was only governments and police forces who could afford them. More than once,

The original 'noddy bike': the hand-start, hand-change LE Velocette.

BMW seriously considered abandoning motorcycle production altogether.

The twins were saved by a clique of far-sighted enthusiasts at the firm, led by Hans-Gunter von der Marwitz, and by a world-wide awakening of interest in Superbikes, really powerful machines of at least 750cc, capable of speeds well in excess of 100 mph. The new 'stroke' series, so called because the first models introduced in 1969 were the R50/5, the R60/5 and the R75/5, were well placed to catch this market and its runners-up. The flagship R75/5 had the same 50 bhp as a Vincent Black Shadow and could cruise at 100 mph, while the R60/5 could hit the 'ton' just about anywhere and the R50/5 could manage three figures on a good day with a following wind. The numbers, for the first time, meant something outside the factory: the 50/5 was a 500 (actually 498cc, 32 bhp), the 60/5 was a 600 (599cc, 40 bhp) and the 75/5 was a 750 (745cc, 50 bhp). These machines turned around BMW's image and fortunes.

The /6 series followed in 1973, with the R60/6, R75/6, R90/6 and R90/S. The two smaller models had the same power output as the /5 series, but the wildly overbored R90/6, 898cc (achieved with a 90 mm bore, because all stroke models shared a 70.6 mm stroke with each other and the motor-car line up) offered 60 bhp and a top speed of about 190 kph (just under 120 mph), while the high-compression /S version of the same motor, with Dell'Ortos instead of Bings, delivered 67 bhp at 7000 rpm, and could

Steib sidecars were the only option for the serious BMW outfit fancier for decades.

98

Moto-Guzzi's baby – a 1983 V35 II.

comfortably exceed 200 kph (124 mph); in fact, a true 130 mph was just about possible.

BMW purists agree that the 90 mm bore was too great and destroyed the smoothness which had always been one of the great attractions of the flat-twin design. While 67 bhp may not seem much nowadays, in its time it was truly remarkable, and it is also worth remembering that these were full-sized DIN horses, not the funny little Japanese ponies which some Oriental manufacturers seem to use. The R90/S was unquestionably one of the first 'hyperbikes', the term coined to go beyond 'superbikes', and in its turn it spawned the R100S and the R100RS. The original R100S of 1976 was basically an R90/S bored to 94 mm (980cc), and it delivered 65 bhp at 6,600 rpm. The faired R100RS, with its brilliant wind-tunnel designed fairing, had 70 bhp at 7250 rpm, and permitted comfortable cruising at 110–120 mph (180–190 kph). What is more, getting down behind the screen and taking the engine up to the rev limit allowed the rider to exceed 130 mph

with ease. The cooking R100/7 had a mere 60 bhp, enough for 115 mph, while the 75/7 and 60/7 continued at 50 bhp and 40 bhp respectively. In due course, the 75/7 was replaced by the 80/7, and the R60/7 gave way to the R45 and R65, in which the venerable twin was redesigned once more. There was also the R80GS off-road bike which, in turn, gave rise to the various R80 derivatives, but for many people (the author included) the R100RS remains the *summa summarum* of the big twins. There is no doubt that modern BMWs are not built the way they used to be: if they were, they would cost twice as much as they do. There is equally no doubt, though, that the design is far more refined than it used to be, which more than makes up for any slight failings in detail and finish.

A later LE Velocette stripped in a desperate attempt to get a decent power-to-weight ratio!

So considerable was the success of the BMW that a whole school of motorcycle design was, (to be charitable) inspired by the Bavarian twin. Even discounting the military pressures which led Harley-Davidson and Zundapp to build BMW lookalikes, the Swiss Condor, the French CEMEC, the Japanese Marusho and the German Windhoff were all clearly BMW-influenced or inspired. There have, however, been some genuinely original flat twins from other manufacturers.

100

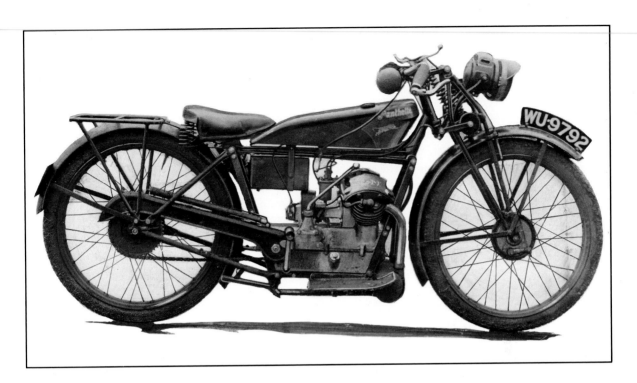

Phelon and Moore's
unsuccessful Panthette.

Douglas's 1935 decision to mount their motors transversely in their Endeavour must have been influenced by BMW, but it would be uncharitable in the extreme to compare them with some of the names above. Douglas were merely taking the logical next step in flat-twin design. Their post-war 350cc bikes are, however, arguably the nicest 'mini-BMWs' ever made. Douglas also showed a touch of Brough Superior influence by designating their 1950 model 350cc flat twin the 90 Plus, a reference to its speed, the name 80 Plus being reserved for those machines which did not quite make it on the dynamometer! Although these post-war Douggies were delightful little bikes, they never made much of an impact on the market, and production gradually waned. The last flat-twin Douglas, the 1954 350cc Dragonfly, was finally 'knocked out' by a London firm of discount dealers in 1958.

Other small transverse twins include the Italian Rocket, a 198cc machine from the 1950s, the 250 and 350cc German Hoffmans from the same period, the Belgian Soicovel – one version of which was powered by a 296cc Coventry-Victor engine, though Coventry-Victor motorcycle production had ceased in 1936 – and the Italian 150cc Capriolo. But the flat twin which went the furthest from the BMW concept was also one of the most successful, and certainly one of the best loved, the LE Velocette.

Velocette were well known for their sporting 350cc and 500cc singles but, after the war, they tried a radical new addition to their line: a 150cc, water-cooled, unit-construction, shaft-drive motorcycle with a hand start, hand change and a pressed steel frame incorporating a good deal of weather protection. It was delightfully quiet, comfortable and reliable, and its only drawback (apart from its weird looks) was its complete and utter gutlessness. Even when the capacity was increased to 192cc the LE was hard put to exceed 45 mph, which was one of the reasons for its reputation for excellent handling: it simply never went fast enough to show up the shortcomings in the frame, though enthusiastic cornering would ground the footboards and produce a fine shower of sparks. The rare Velocette Valiant, an air-cooled ohv version with a more conventional frame and appearance, was introduced in 1957 but did little more than confirm manufacturers (and the public's) prejudice against small, fancy engines: it was still completely gutless, though very pretty.

The Velocette LE did, however, find many friends among the police where it became the well-known 'Noddy Bike', in use for urban patrols, and all who owned or rode LEs tend to remember them with affection. With detail changes, such as the adoption of a kick starter and a foot change, the LE ran from 1948 to around 1968, not a bad production run for a bike widely regarded (not least by its makers) as a failure.

As the LE's life was drawing to a close, and as BMW prepared to revitalise their motorcycles with the /5 series, another transverse-engined motorcycle was waiting in the wings. It was built around an engine originally designed to power an ultra-lightweight cross-country vehicle for the Italian Army, and which had actually been used in a wildly improbable half-tracked tricycle which looked like a cross between a *Kettenrad* and a Servi-Car. It came from the old-established firm of Moto-Guzzi, who in 1966 were in dire financial straits and had just been taken over by Alejandro de Tomaso, an Argentine-born Italian who has almost single-handedly turned around the Italian motorcycle industry.

The Moto-Guzzi V twin has been likened, with some justice, to a BMW with the cylinders bent upwards. It first appeared in 703cc guise in 1967, with either 35 bhp at 5000 rpm in the soft-tuned Polizia guise (it was originally conceived as a police motorcycle), or 40 bhp at 5800 rpm as the standard V7. The performance was similar to that of the BMW R60/5, which appeared a couple of years later, but the handling was if anything rather sweeter.

Predictably, a V7 Special version appeared a couple of years later (in 1969) with an extra 44cc, and 45 bhp at 6000 rpm. The new 747cc motor was fitted into the Special sports bike, and into a de-luxe tourer called the Ambassador and, in 1971, it appeared in the first California, a grand tourer in the American fashion. Some idea of the torque available can be gauged from the fact that the quoted top speeds of all these machines are the same, at 170 kph (105 mph).

It was in 1971 that a choice of engine sizes first became available, with either a 748cc V7 Sport or an 844cc California, and the number of gears available grew to five. The new V7 Sport offered 52 bhp at 6300 rpm, but by virtue of its light weight and slim profile could touch the magic 200 kph (124 mph), while the California, in a softer state of tune and with much more weight and frontal area, could only manage 175 kph (109 mph).

In 1972, the 850 motor was inserted into the V850 GT, which was

The Moto-Guzzi 850 T5 may look dated next to its Japanese contemporaries – but who could deny it classic status?

supposed to be good for 180 kph (112 mph), but by 1974 the same engine had been persuaded to disburse 59 bhp at 6800 rpm, which allowed the 850T to exceed 180 kph and even propelled the mighty footboard-equipped California T3 at that speed. In the same year the 750 S and 750 S3 gained another couple of horsepower, making 200 kph a certainty instead of something requiring a bit of luck, and the venerable 850 was pushed to 71 bhp. The more powerful motor first appeared in the V 850 Le Mans, a bigger, heavier motorcycle than the 750 but with more acceleration and a slightly more relaxed way of delivering it. Subsequent developments of the 850 motor have been the 73 bhp version used in the 850 Le Mans III since 1981, and the 60 bhp versions used for tourers. It is no great surprise that 73 bhp should be the limit reached so far, as BMW reckoned that 67 bhp was the most they could wring from the 900, and 70 bhp was the maximum for reliable running with the 980cc boxer. It is also whispered that the Italian firm's claims are not quite so conservative as the Bavarians', so the actual power outputs are not dissimilar.

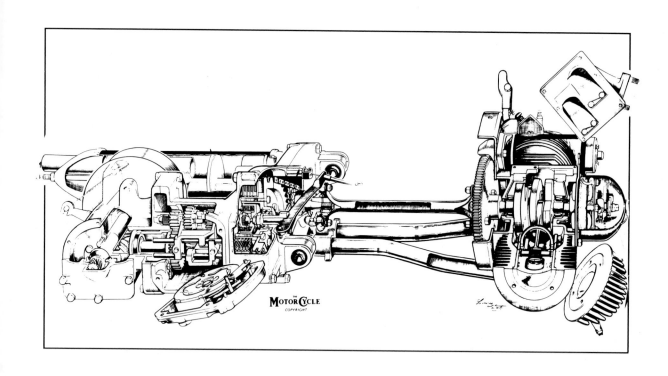

THE MOTOR CYCLE
COPYRIGHT

There proved, however, to be room to extract another 105cc from the long-suffering Italian lump, and the so-called 1000cc (actually 949cc) version was used to provide a softer-tuned, more tractable version of the big twin. It first appeared in 1975, with 61 bhp, in the V1000 I Convert which was a massive tourer, with a two-speed *automatic* gearbox, but enough torque to allow a top speed of 175 kph (109 mph) even with this handicap. I must confess that I have never ridden this machine, but I know that owners (as distinct from journalists) have spoken highly of it. When it next appeared, in the V1000 G5 in 1978, it had 63 bhp and a conventional gearbox. It also appeared with the same power output in the 1000 California II in 1982. Curiously, the same top speed is claimed for all of these machines, but I should not care to race a Convert against a G5.

With the success of the big engine, the ingenious gentlemen at Mandello del Lario turned their minds to producing a smaller version of the same thing. It would not have been possible to produce quite the same engine in a smaller size, as scaling down never works, but the idea of a 90° transverse V twin was still there.

The engine appeared in 1977 on the V50, a beautiful little 490cc motorcycle with 45 bhp and a top speed of just a whisker over 100 mph.

Changes to the engine included the adoption of Nikasil-type light alloy cylinders, and the whole machine was ideal for smaller riders or for those who simply liked small motorcycles. In Italy, a 346cc version (called, predictably, the V35) was also introduced in the same year in order to take advantage of tax breaks. With only 33.5 bhp, the V35's performance was necessarily less impressive than that of the V50, but it was still a very pleasant little machine. It was introduced in different countries at different times, Britain being one of the last beneficiaries (at least in the normal motorcycle buying world) in 1984.

The V50 and V35 were the first of a new generation of mass-produced European motorcycles expressly designed to compete with the Japanese on more-or-less equal terms though, in terms of handling, it was widely agreed that the Italians had an easy lead. A particularly interesting feature of all current Moto-Guzzi V-twins is the provision of linked braking, whereby the foot brake operates not only the rear disc, as is normal, but also one of the front discs, with the braking effort split 60% front, 40% rear. The hand brake operates the other front disc. Once again, journalists have sometimes been rude about this system. While there is little doubt that for ultimate control by top riders the braking systems should be separate, the linked brakes are no disadvantage for even the skilled rider, and can be a major advantage. There were, however, real problems with the finish, which was frankly patchy and which has only recently taken a turn for the better. Later models of the V50 (the II and III) still used the 45 bhp engine, but the V50 Monza (1981) was a 'go-faster' faired version with an extra 3 bhp and slightly increased top speed. The equivalent V35 was the V35 Imola (1980), with 36 bhp and a top speed in sight of 100 mph, and only a very slight incline or tail wind was needed to reach the magic ton. There were also 'custom' versions of both the V35 and V50, both slower and more tiring to ride than their straight counterparts, but appealing to those who prefer looks to all else.

At the time of writing, the latest manifestation of Moto-Guzzi's baby V twin is the 643cc/52 bhp V65, which possesses a similar top speed to the original 750cc and even 850cc machines, much better acceleration and a tremendous degree of 'flickability'. The V65 and V65 SP are both good for almost 110 mph (and indeed indicate that speed quite regularly, because of the slightly optimistic speedometers normally fitted) whilst the V65 Custom is, as usual, a few miles an hour slower. The latest version of the bigger machine, at the time of writing, is the Moto-Guzzi Le Mans 4, which (to be truthful) is very similar to the previous model. The big V twin is beginning to look very dated, though sales are still surprisingly good.

9
Stevenage Vincit Omnia

When you look at a Vincent V-twin it is hard not to see it as a huge and beautiful engine to which someone has bolted the minimum number of components necessary to turn it into a motorcycle. Like all great machinery, it has its foibles – more than one would-be rider has literally been thrown into the air trying to start it – but it also has some extraordinary qualities.

For years it was the fastest production motorcycle. This alone would qualify it as one of the all-time greats. In addition to this, it was designed from the very start to be unbelievably reliable. The intention was to make a machine which would cover 100,000 miles between major overhauls. If anything did go wrong it was to be such a simple machine to work on that a very modest tool kit would suffice for a complete overhaul. In those happy days it was assumed that the rider would want to do most of the maintenance

Vincent Series B Rapide.

The Plumber's Nightmare –
Series A Rapide.

himself: there were no special tools or 'workshop only' procedures. And finally, Philip C Vincent wanted the motorcycle which bore his name to be affordable, which marks it out from the other British V-twin superbikes, the Brough Superior and the Hesketh, which were both avowedly expensive.

It was this insistence on affordability which probably killed the Vincent in the end: that, and the fact that enthusiasts seldom make the best business-men, because they are so obsessed with their own vision of perfection that they do not make the commercial compromises that are necessary to survive. Consequently, the history of the Vincent is short but tangled.

Once upon a time, there was successful TT rider called Howard Raymond Davis. To capitalise upon his name and his knowledge, he founded the firm of HRD Motorcycles in 1924. In 1925 he won the Senior TT on one of his own machines, and in 1927 Freddie Dixon won the Junior on another. They were rigid-framed bikes with JAP single-cylinder engines, their only noticeably modern feature being saddle tanks, but they were certainly successful in competition. Unfortunately, Davis was not as good a business-man as he was a rider, and his company went into liquidation shortly after Freddie Dixon's win.

Philip C Vincent, generally known as PCV, had been a motorcyclist since his teens. While still at school he had built a 350cc special with an unusually strong rear-sprung frame of his own invention. At Cambridge he had ridden

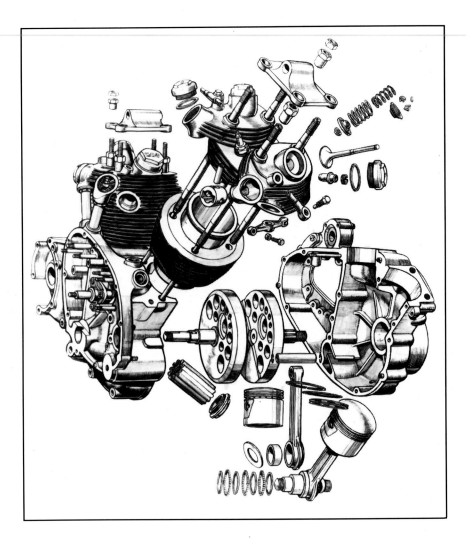

a friend's McEvoy-Anzani, and by the late 1920s he knew exactly what sort of motorcycle he wanted to build himself. With backing from his father, a wealthy rancher in Argentina, he bought the HRD name together with a certain amount of HRD knowledge and spare parts, hired several ex-HRD personnel, and found premises. The whole exercise cost £30,000, £400 for the HRD name, the rest to set up the business. At that time, there were $4 US to the £ sterling, so the dollar equivalents were $1600 for the name and $120,000 overall.

The original Vincent HRD was offered with a choice of MAG or JAP singles in an unusual sprung frame of PCV's own design. Literally hinged in the middle, it was derived from the frame he had designed for his original special, and it was to be the basis of all subsequent Vincent V-twins and big singles, albeit in much abbreviated form in its later incarnations. To say that the machine was 'offered' accurately reflects the limited response which it engendered. In the first year of trading only 24 machines were sold, many to old Cambridge friends. One of the few that was sold, however, was taken on a round-the-world tour, and when the pillion passenger decided that he had had enough, in Australia, his place was taken by a young man called Phil Irving.

Phil Irving was to become a legend. To this day, his book *Motorcycle Engineering* is regarded by many as the basic text on the subject. He was also to become heavily involved with the Vincent HRD Company. It was he who tidied up the frame (though it had already been redesigned once, before he joined the firm, in 1931), and it was he who was mostly responsible for the 500cc Vincent single-cylinder engine which was built for the 1934 season, after a particularly disastrous experience with a JAP engine had persuaded PCV to develop an engine of his own.

The 500cc single was built with an eye to simplicity and home maintenance, but also with performance in mind. The high-mounted cam and short push-rods were described (not entirely accurately) as 'semi overhead cam', and allowed high crankshaft speeds, as did the relatively short stroke 84 × 90 mm engine. Previous Vincent-HRDs had been good for something over 80 mph; the new bike could hit 90 with ease, and the 1936 Comet Special with bronze head, increased compression ratio (8:1) and a larger carburettor could exceed 100 mph, and frequently did.

It was the 500cc single which formed the basis for the V-twin. Phil Irving noticed two drawings lying on top of one another, overlapped the crank cases more precisely and realised that it should be possible to built a 1000cc V-twin from two 500cc top ends and a new bottom end. Of course, translating this idea into metal was not easy, but it was far from impossible, and the prototype Vincent Rapide was built as a $47\frac{1}{2}°$ vee, with the rear cylinder offset $1\frac{1}{4}$ inches to allow side-by-side con-rods (instead of a 'knife and fork') and to assist cooling of the rear cylinder. The reason for the odd angle was sheer production expediency; the engine was built to fit into a special frame, which had been ordered to take a JAP V-twin, but which had never been collected by the customer.

The original 'plumber's nightmare' was so called because of the profusion of external oil-pipes, a carry-over from the 500cc single, but all the more obvious because there were twice as many cylinders and apparently more than twice as many pipes. All these oil-pipes did, however, have one important consequence. Because the whole machine – including the top-end valve gear – was correctly lubricated, it was inherently built to last. Bear in mind that at the time this machine was introduced, there were still many motorcyclists who had been brought up on total-loss hand-oilers.

It was a rip-roaring motorcycle. To modern eyes 45 bhp from a 998cc engine may not seem remarkable; but combined with the immense torque of the big low-compression (6.6:1) engine, a slim profile, and an overall weight of about 430 lb (under 200 kg), it was enough to wind the machine up to around 110 mph in top (fourth) gear, with 80 mph available in second and nearly 100 mph in third. The bike had its drawbacks, though. It spat oil in the finest British tradition, and the bought-in Burman clutch and gearbox were simply not up to the job. Only 78 of these mighty motorcycles were

110

Black crank cases (and more power!) distinguish the Shadow from the Rapide.

built before the war changed everyone's priorities, so pre-war Rapides can hardly be said to have changed the face of motorcycling. Like the singles that had gone before, however, they were an essential stage in the evolution of the post-war Vincents, which for many people were the most desirable motorcycles ever made.

The plans for the post-war machines were laid down during the war. Although Phil Irving had left Vincent for Velocette in 1936, PCV invited him back during the war to be the Works Chief Engineer and to co-design the new machine in the meanwhile. The most obvious difference between the pre-war and post-war V-twin was that the front down-tube of the frame disappeared, replaced by the immensely strong engine as a stressed part of the structure of the motorcycle, in the fashion of the long-established Phelon and Moore Panther. The top tube, in turn, became not only a spine frame member but also the oil tank; it was a massive welded box-section. The rear suspension remained much the same as before, with the large empty space

111

Series B Shadow engine.

under the saddle occupied only by the springs and shock absorber between the rear sprung section and the main frame-cum-engine unit. This is visually odd, particularly to anyone brought up on modern motorcycles with their side-panels and big air boxes, and it was accentuated by the dual seat, which somehow made the space look even emptier than separate seat and pillion would have done. It was this, more than anything else, which gave the Vincent the appearance of being a few cycle parts bolted onto a motor.

The engine was also cleaned up visually, with internal oilways replacing the 'plumber's nightmare', though this was only part of the substantial redesign which included raising the angle between the cylinders to 50°. This was partly a matter of manufacturing expediency, in that it was easier to machine this angle with the tools they had on hand, and partly to accommodate the standard Lucas magneto. Losing the front down-tube made it possible to increase the included angle without increasing the wheelbase (which was, in fact, reduced from $58\frac{1}{2}$ to 56 inches), and even this small an increase materially assisted cooling.

Series B Rapide engine. The clutch and gearbox were also redesigned, as they had to be in order to handle the torque of the new motor (or the old one, for that matter). The clutch was an ingenious self-servo design, with a single-plate pilot clutch and a power clutch which resembled a twin-leading-shoe drum brake. This made two-fingered clutch operation easy, despite the fact that the clutch was said to be able to handle 120 bhp, but the only problem was that the clutch seals were not always entirely oil-tight, so that more than one Vincent owner was acutely embarrassed by well-lubricated clutch linings which refused to transmit all (or, in extreme cases, any) of the engine's power to the rear wheel. The four-speed gearbox, for its part, was designed to have a service life of over 300,000 miles, so there were no problems in that department.

The Series B Rapide, as it was known, appeared in 1946. It was a bit heavier than the original, at 455 lbs, but still a hundred pounds lighter than many Japanese machines of two or three decades later, and still admirably slim. In order to run on the rotten 'pool' petrol of the time, the compression ratio was a very modest 6.45:1, so the quoted power was still only 45 bhp, the

same as the Series A. It was, however, a very much more civilised motorcycle, and as long as the gearbox oil seals held out it was also vastly more reliable.

The Series A and Series B Rapides were very desirable motorcycles, but PCV was still not content. He wanted something even better. The pre-war Comet 500cc single had been hotted up to give 100 mph, and what PCV wanted was a hotted up Rapide.

Frank Walker, the Managing Director of Vincent-HRD, was opposed to

The Black Prince, as ridden by the Thought Police in the original film of 1984, was a fully-enclosed version of the Shadow.

114

the project. One of Walker's functions was to act as a brake upon some of PCV's wilder enthusiasms so, without Walker's knowledge, PCV went ahead and assembled two prototype super-sports V-twins, with Comet cams, blueprinted and polished internals, 7.3:1 compression ratio, and a dramatic black-enamelled engine. As if the mighty engine was not enough, the standard 3-inch, 120 mph speedometer of the Rapide was replaced with a 5-inch, 150 mph model. There was still no rev counter, as it was assumed that any motorcyclist who bought such a machine would be able to judge gear changes by ear. The Black Shadow was born, a name that still sends a chill down the spine of anyone who dreamed of buying a Vincent before they moved out of the realms of motorcycles and into the realms of collectables. A good Series B Black Shadow could just hit 125 mph in newly-fettled condition, and 120 mph was almost commonplace.

Out of the Shadow grew an even more legendary motorcycle, the Black Lightning. The original was built as a 'special' for an attempt on the American speed record for a road-going motorcycle, then held at 136 mph by a much-modified Harley-Davidson. The rider for the record attempt, Rollie Free, was a rugged individualist. He topped 150 mph, lying full length on the machine and wearing nothing but swimming trunks and running shoes. In more coventional attire and position, he still recorded 148 mph and most riders could hope to see 140 mph or more on the clock, without allowance for speedometer optimism. The production Lightning was offered in 1948, with a whole host of racing goodies including hot cams, high compression pistons, bigger carbs, straight through pipes, a racing magneto and alloy wheel rims. It cost over £500, compared with £400 for the Shadow and £336 odd for the Rapide, both of which were now in Series C guise.

The Series C Vincents, which ran from 1948 to 1953 inclusive, are the definitive Vinnies for most people. Even the cooking Series C Rapide was a very quick motorcycle, and as you rose from this through the Shadow to the Lightning specifications, power rose from 45 bhp to 55 bhp to around 70 bhp. By contrast, the weight rose only 3 lb from the Rapide to the Shadow (that massive speedometer must have had something to do with it!), and then fell dramatically to well under 400 lb for the extensively stripped and drilled Lightning, which was never intended to be used as a road bike, though (inevitably) some were appropriately modified.

The best seller was the Shadow, representing for most people a tremendous combination of practicality (which the Lightning somewhat lacked) and performance. Most road testers got Series Cs well into the 120s, and often nearer 130 than 120 mph. The Shadow was, however, an idiosyncratic motorcycle which was both over- and under-priced. The vagaries of the clutch have already been mentioned, and the curious-looking Girdraulic forks were extremely effective but rather out of – to be fair, ahead of – the mainstream. During the life of the Series C, several components were reduced in specification to save money. The new parts usually worked every bit as well as the old, but were more susceptible to 'bodgery' and ham-fistedness during repair, so the Vincent reputation for reliability began to

The 120 mph clock on the Rapide is replaced with a massive 5-inch, 150 mph version on the Shadow.

suffer just slightly. As for the price, it was too high to find a really wide market but too low to be adequately profitable. The writing was already on the wall, and after Phil Irving left the company to go back to Australia in 1949 it became even more clearly readable. The company also suffered a terrible stroke of bad luck when the Argentine government imposed currency controls which not only stopped PCV's father from injecting more capital into the company, but also led to the loss of potentially very profitable sales of Vincents to the Argentine police and services.

The all-enclosed Black Knight (Rapide specification engine) and Black Prince (Shadow spec, 55 bhp motor) which appeared in 1954 did nothing to improve the company's fortunes. There is no doubt that they were fascinating machines with superbly-finished fibreglass bodywork; and the twin aims of weather protection and easy cleaning were brilliantly realised. But they were too advanced for the conservatively-minded motorcyclist, indeed, they would probably be too advanced today, and the Series D Rapide had to be introduced in 1955 in a desperate attempt to win back the market. The Series D showed evidence of cost savings in many areas: the tommy-bar arrangement for removing the wheels went (though this did discourage thieves); the chain adjusters were replaced with a conventional nut-and-bolt type; the seat stays and friction dampers were omitted; and the price in 1955 was fractionally less than it had been in 1953. Very few Vincent Series D motorcycles were made, as production ceased in 1955.

Overall, the Vincent lived up to its designer's hopes. It was the fastest production motorcycle available in its time; it was easy to work on; it was superbly reliable (with one reservation about the clutch oil seals); and it has become a legend. What might not have happened if PCV had been as much of a businessman as he was a motorcyclist? It can fairly be said, as an epitaph, that Vincents are to the world of classic motorcycling what Leicas are to camera collectors: the word 'fanatical' is hardly strong enough to convey the enthusiasm Vincents engender, and when you ride one, it is not hard to see why.

10
The Italian Job

The Italian motorcycle industry, like the Italian automobile industry, has always been torn between sport and utility. In a few cases they manage to combine the two, but in most cases the difference is striking: a Vespa scooter versus a Laverda triple, a Fiat 500 versus a Maserati. There is also a rich vein of mechanical inventiveness verging upon eccentricity, as witness Moto-Guzzi's V8 racer.

With three notable road-going exceptions, and one racer, the V-twin has not been a typically Italian configuration. Why this should be the case is not entirely clear, unless it is the Italian taxation laws, which traditionally have penalised big engines quite disproportionately. Another possibility is that the V-twin has not, since the 1920s, been regarded as the ultimate racing machine: maximum power per cubic centimetre came first from highly-developed singles, and then from in-line multis with ever-increasing numbers of cylinders (the first production in-line 'six' came from Benelli). The

Ducati's 750 Desmo – pour le sport.

Italian fondness for speed is proverbial, and a racing heritage, or at least appearance, sells motorcycles.

One of the road-going bikes, the Moto-Guzzi has already been considered in Chapter 8. As we have seen, it is somewhat out of the mainstream of Italian motorcycle development. Although the Spada and Le Mans versions were decently fast in their day, the most successful bikes were always the more comfortable and civilised tourers, especially the massive 750, 850 and 1000cc versions. And who would have thought that the Italians would have fitted automatic transmission to a real motor-cycle, as distinct from a moped?

The racing exception, the 120° Moto-Guzzi 500cc of the mid-1930s, won the Senior TT in 1935 at an average speed of 84.68 mph. Mounted conventionally (longitudinally) in the frame, it allowed a very low centre of gravity and a slightly shorter wheelbase than a flat twin of the same capacity and disposition, as well as cooling the rear cylinder more effectively than a longitudinal flat twin, however, it was still something of a dead-end in the technical development of the V-twin. It was interesting, but (apart from its success in the TT) not very significant.

There are, though, two Italian V-twins which positively scream their origins. They have all the hallmarks of Italian motor-cycles: superb engines, impeccable handling and variable finish, poor electrics, arse-numbing sporting seats, and often a total disregard for air filtration. In fact, finish has improved dramatically over the last few years, and the electrics are by no means as bad as they used to be, but there is no doubt that these are sports motorcycles of a particularly uncompromising nature. They are Ducati and Moto Morini.

Both V-twins were children of the 1970s, although Moto Morini's history goes back to 1937 and Ducati's (at least as a motorcycle manufacturer) to the immediately post-WW2 period. The Ducati came first, at the Milan show in 1970, while the Morini was introduced to the public at the same venue, three years later.

The Ducati is markedly the less conventional of the two. In first place, it is a 90° conventionally-mounted twin, and in the second place, desmodromic valve control has been standard on many models.

Although a 90° V-twin necessarily implies a fairly long wheelbase, the designer (Ing Taglioni) managed to keep it to a reasonable 60 inches by a number of expedient moves. The front cylinder protrudes through the frame, and is almost parallel with the ground (the engine is canted backwards by 15°), whilst the gearbox has been shortened by stacking the mainshaft and layshaft one above the other. Because of the configuration chosen, cooling was inherently good, and it was assisted still further by the 25 mm offset of the cylinders, by the use of coil (instead of hairpin) valve-springs on non-desmodromic versions in order to keep the rocker boxes narrow, and by the initially odd-looking finning, which runs parallel to the bore on the front cylinder and at right angles to it on the rear cylinder.

Desmodromic valve control is still sufficiently rare to warrant explaining. On most four-stroke engines the valves are positively opened (by the cam-

The Ducati at the end of the rainbow – a 1984 900S2.

lobe itself, or by a rocker arm), and closed by a spring. Although this is admirably simple, the trouble with it is that at very high engine speeds the valves begin to 'float', because their inertia is such that the spring simply cannot close them before the piston rises to TDC on the next stroke. The result is a collision between the two, a bent or broken valve and a greater or lesser mechanical disintegration of the engine. The more usual approach to this problem is the adoption of multiple valves, which reduce the inertia of each individual valve and make it easier to close – the classic four valve head – but an alternative is to open *and close* the valves positively, which is the meaning of 'desmodromic' valve control.

Very few manufacturers have ever experimented with desmodromics, and the only notable successes have been the Mercedes racing-car engines of the early 1950s, and several Ducati designs since about 1955. The ultimate Ducati Desmo designs employed no fewer than three cam-shafts, two for opening and one for closing the valves, but a rather simpler design with one

cam-shaft per cylinder was adopted for the V-twin Desmo designs. The result of adopting the system is that the engines are very costly and mechanically complicated to make, but that they can achieve quite extra-ordinary speeds for a given engine displacement. The advantages in racing are self-evident, but for a road bike the result is both increased power and a remarkable margin of safety for over-revving.

The 90° angle and desmodromic valve control are not the only examples of no compromise engineering, either. The gear-driven overhead cams are a striking feature, as is the geared primary drive. Like the Vincent, the Ducati is basically an engine first, and a motorcycle second. The original 750cc version was reputed to produce 50 bhp at the rear wheel, 20% more at the crankshaft, which by the standards of 1970 was no mean power output. This bike was, however, a traditional sporting motorcycle. Although it sported 12v electrics (even at that late date, something of an innovation in Italy), there was no electric starter: *machismo* kicking was the order of the day. Both seat and suspension were rock-hard. It was not a bike to appeal to those used to luxury, or even comfort, but it did go and it did turn corners. Remember, the Japanese at that time were still firmly of the 'hinge in the middle' persuasion when it came to motorcycle manufacturing.

The original 750 went through several stages in gaining power. The 1972 750 Sport was, like the 1970 model, a valve-spring motor. But increasing the

The engineering is Italian – but the styling, curiously enough, is British on the Hailwood Replica.

compression ratio to 9:1 from 8.5:1, omitting the air cleaners and using 32 mm accelerator-pump Dell Ortos gave 56 bhp at the rear wheel at 8200 rpm, 500 rpm faster than the basic model. Then, in 1972, the full-blown Desmo model appeared. Called the 750SS (for Super Sport), the cams were profiled for increased lift and overlap, and around 65 bhp was available at the rear wheel. The whole engine was breathed upon, with extensive crack-testing, blueprinting, polishing, shimming, etc and primary gears straight-cut instead of helical. Three cast-iron Brembos (280 mm at the front, 225 mm at the rear) took care of braking, at least in the dry, and the whole plot was very quick indeed at 135 mph plus. In truth, it was a real road/racer, and more racer than road: noisy, ferocious and built only with speed and handling in mind, it was a bike which tempted its riders to do silly things. In the rain, the brakes were dubious, the finish fell off and the electrics failed, but in fair weather it was a stunning motorcycle.

The classic way to get more power is more cubes, and in 1973 the 860 GTI appeared in the usual way, at the Milan show. This bike was never actually produced in its show form, but appeared in early 1975 as the 860 GT. The extra capacity was achieved by a 6mm increase in bore. The 860 was, however, detectably softer than the old 750s. Weight had increased by over 20 lb, and the silencers now lived up to their name, coming from Lanfranconi instead of Conti, so it was not until a desmodromic version of this motor appeared that real Ducati addicts could rely on a new fix. Called the 900SS (although the capacity was exactly the same as the 860), it delivered 68 bhp at the rear wheel at 7000 rpm; power dropped off steadily after 7200 rpm, but the rev limit was effectively 8000 rpm for those who wanted to rake their engines, or for racers. For a V-twin of this capacity, this represented (and represents) a truly remarkable limit. The 900SS was good for a genuine 140 mph, and if the racing pack which the factory offered was fitted, the result was awesome.

A derated version of the 900SS, the Darmah, still used desmodromic valve control but gave ten fewer horsepower at the rear wheel and offered electric starting as standard, an option grudgingly introduced some time before on the bottom-of-the-line 750cc bikes, but still regarded as too effeminate for the 'real' sports models. The Darmah appeared in 1976. The only other really noteworthy big Duke since then has been the so-called Hailwood Replica introduced in 1979. Dressed up as a racer to look like the one which Hailwood rode so successfully at the Isle of Man in 1978, it is actually a standard 900SS under the fairing and paint job, and it is reputed to be fractionally slower than the 'undressed' bike, but its looks are quite stunning. At the time of writing, the promised 1000cc Ducati had not appeared, and in view of Ducati's tie-up with Cagiva – of which more, later – there were still some people not entirely sure that it would.

Meanwhile, back at the ranch, Ing Taglioni had devised a smaller V-twin, the Pantah. Scaling down the bevel-gear OHC would have resulted in an absurdly expensive small engine, and so a toothed-belt drive was adopted to the SOHC – but desmodromic valve operation was retained as standard, instead of being reserved only for the go-faster versions. The result of this design was a light, fast-revving 500cc engine, which could deliver just under 50 bhp (measured at the rear wheel) at 9000 rpm. There were several other changes when compared with the bigger engines; plain big-end shells replaced roller-bearings – and necessitated much higher lube-feed pressures, achieved with a gear-type pump – and Gilnisil lining was used in the light-alloy bores instead of conventional iron liners. An act of near-heresy was the provision of electric starting as standard, without even the option of a kick-start, but the result as revealed in 1979 was the fastest 500cc bike on the road, with 200 kph (124 mph) just attainable, provided the rider was well tucked in, with his head behind the screen – about the same as a contemporary BMW of twice the capacity, albeit without fairing!

Once again, the Pantah was designed as a sporting machine with few concessions to anything except speed and handling, and it was not a bike on which most people would have cared to go touring. Once again the finish was not brilliant (though Ducati was improving steadily), and the electrics did attract criticism. But for a rider who simply wanted to ride . . .

The Pantah 500 begat the Pantah 600 in 1981, bored out to give 583cc and about another 3 bhp at the rear wheel, plus considerably more bottom-end torque. Almost any rider could now rely on a genuine 125 mph, and 130 mph was not out of sight in the right conditions. In 1982, a smaller Pantah also

The first big Cagivas were Ducati-powered V-twins. This is a 1984 650 model.

appeared, a mere 349cc tiddler designed to fit into one of the numerous Italian tax classes with as little room to spare as possible. The Pantah 350, despite its desmodromic valve operation, offered only 35 bhp at the rear wheel, but that was still enough to permit a genuine ton under almost any conditions, with 105 mph a realistic maximum.

At the time of writing, the latest Ducati V-twin to appear is actually a Cagiva. The Cagiva company has been involved in a number of complex negotiations, which no-one seems to understand too well, with Ducati. These have led to rumours that big Dukes will disappear altogether, or that they will only appear under the Cagiva label, but (as already mentioned) the announcement of a 1000cc Ducati, under the Ducati tank badge, seems to scotch at least some of those rumours. What is certain is that the Cagiva 650 is powered by a bored and stroked version of the Pantah engine, and one which also appears in a Ducati in some markets. The maximum bhp seems to be another 3–4 bhp higher than the 583cc engine, but again with more torque, and revised gearing for better acceleration below 100–110 mph at the expense of a top speed slightly lower than the 600 Ducati. What is also certain is that the Alazzura, as the Cagiva is called, is fractionally more civilised than the Ducati. It has more flexible suspension, a better-padded seat and a footrest/bar/seat layout that does not force the rider into an uncompromising racing crouch, like it or not.

It may well be that the different philosophies of the two companies will allow two different model lines to be developed, a raw-edged road-racer for Ducati (at which they have always excelled), and a rather softer roadster for Cagiva, a type of bike which has never been very successful for Ducati. It is also possible that the end is drawing nigh for desmodromic V-twins, though this does not seem likely. Whatever the truth it seems likely that the ultimate, classic Ducatis are now in the past, killed by noise regulations and construction-and-use regulations rather than by any short comings in their design. No matter how good Ducatis and Cagivas may be in the future, we shall not see the like of those road-racers again, at least not in dealers' showrooms.

The word that is most often used of Moto Morini, the other classic Italian V-twin, is *different*, and different it certainly is. Alfonso Morini was first associated with the MM company, founded in 1924, and in 1937 he left to set up a new company under his own name. The war intervened, and it was not until 1946 that the first machine bearing the Morini label – a 123cc two-stroke – appeared on the market. Between then and 1973, the Morini factory

The European Racing Elephant is a little-known breed, but attracts new admirers every season.

produced a number of very fast two-stroke and four-stroke single-cylinder 'tiddlers', including several double overhead cam designs. The very biggest Morinis were only 246cc (albeit 246cc racers capable of over 135 mph), and the range extended down to 48cc.

At the 1973 Milan motor show, some four years after Alfonso's death, Morini introduced their first V-twin, and their biggest motorcycle to date, with a 344cc motor. This engine, with its 72° included angle and *désaxé* cylinders, has already been mentioned in Chapter One; suffice to say here that it also ran (and runs) an indecently high compression ratio (11.2:1, on the 500cc version) which was made possible by the Heron head and bowl-in-piston combustion chamber. This allowed over 100 bhp/litre from a push-rod engine: 35 bhp at 8200 rpm in cooking form, or 39 bhp in sports tune. Inevitably, the power was a little peaky, and the 5-speed gearbox had to be used in order to keep the engine on the cam, but with a dry weight of under 170 Kg (370 1b), it was enough for quite sparkling performance. A hundred mph was available on any reasonable straight, and as one might expect from a firm with such a high commitment to racing, the handling was superb and, surprisingly, the machine was introduced with air cleaners as standard, and an electric foot, which marked it out as a bike which the manufacturers had actually contemplated being ridden on the road as a practical motorcycle. And the roads which it liked, and on which it was really at home, were the twisting, turning, rising and falling ones in the country rather than the

Cagiva leaves you in no doubt that the rev counter is more important than the speedo – good racing practice.

autostrade or motorways, which suited the crazy Italian speed-limit laws very well; these are so weird that they are worth describing in detail.

In Italy, speed limits vary according to engine capacity. On *autostrade*, the speed limit for any motorcycle over 149cc is 130 kph (82 mph), the same as for cars of 900–1300cc, whereas for larger cars, the limit is 140 kph (88 mph). On ordinary roads, however, the speed limit for bikes remains the same, whilst for even the largest cars it drops to 110 kph (68 mph). Of course, the law is little observed, and virtually unenforceable anyway, but it does explain why riding motorcycles on ordinary roads in Italy is even more fun than riding them on *autostrade*.

The 350cc capacity also marks a break-point in the Italian taxation and insurance rates, which makes this an attractive engine size for the home market, so it was no surprise that Morini opted for it and did well; but there is always a demand for more of a good thing, and so in 1977 came a 500cc version of the same bike, only a little heavier but with 479cc instead of 344cc and about 10 more bhp, bringing a genuine 110 mph within reach and making 100 mph an everyday occurrence instead of requiring a bit of a run-up.

On this point (of Morini speeds) it is worth stating that the bikes do need to be carefully run in for a long way, if they are to deliver their best performance. Independent road-testers have often been unable to persuade even the 500cc version to exceed 100 mph across a timed distance, but *Inside Morini's 350cc gem.*

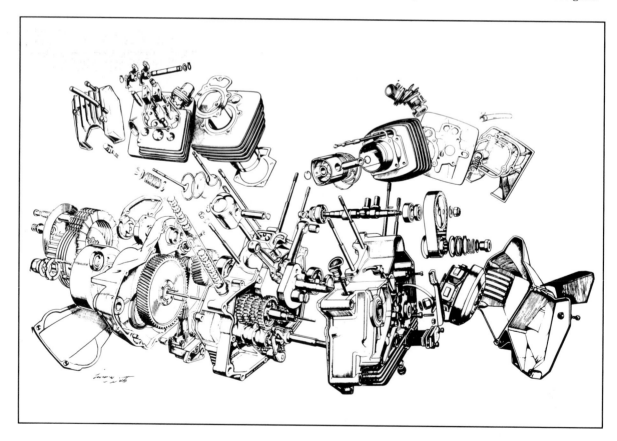

126

*Morini's classic 350 V-twin;
this is a 1984 model.*

reading their reports a little more closely usually reveals some such comment as 'a rather tight new engine, which loosened up considerably during the test ...', in other words, an engine which had been methodically raked by journalists from new. Harglo, the English importers, recommend no less than 4000 miles of gradually increasing speeds and acceleration before the bike is fully run in and, of course, a small engine like this is bound to need more careful running in than (say) a Hesketh, where the power available is so massive that it is no great hardship to take things easy and stay below 80 or 90 mph for a couple of thousand miles, or to refrain from 13-second standing quarters.

Rather more of a surprise was the introduction of a 250cc version of the same bike in 1979. With considerably less performance than the bigger versions, a top speed only just in excess of 80 mph, the 250 was apparently aimed at those who wanted Morini handling, but lower insurance rates. As with the 350cc and 500cc bikes, the performance on paper does not tell the whole story, and one Morini rider of my acquaintance who commutes daily to New York City from his home in the hills nearly 50 miles away can tell some delightful stories of beating Japanese behemoths on the twisty bits on any one of his three Morinis: like a number of the more manic Morini owners, he actually has a full set, the 250cc, 350cc and 500cc.

Admittedly, he only has one version of each capacity, and there are now (for example) three versions of the 350: the cooking version, the sports version and (believe it or not) an off-road version, sold in some countries as the Camel and in others as the Sahara. There is also a 500cc version of the off-road bike, which was introduced in 1980/81, and this is the more popular version in those countries where there is no great tax advantage to a 350cc motorcycle. Built to catch the 'Paris-Dakar Poseur' market, which is very strong in a number of European countries, the Camel/Sahara is apparently a much better off-road bike than its racing heritage might lead one to believe, but it is still regarded with suspicion by many 'real' Morini riders, who believe in the Pure Gospel of the Numb Backside, and tend to ride very quickly in the very early hours of the morning, before the police wake up.

There is no doubt that the Morini rider marches (or at least rides) to a different drum, and that it is not a drum which all can hear, let alone follow, but for a supremely sporting motorcycle which is ridden purely for its own sake, rather than as a means of getting from A to B or even as a means of going at particularly high speeds, the Morini has few equals.

Both ends, but not the middle: Morini's biggest and smallest V-twins.

11
Rule Britannia

The Hesketh is, by any standards, an anachronism. Massively over-engineered, high-priced and virtually custom-built for each buyer, it seems more at home in the 1920s than in the 1980s. It is tempting to think that if George Brough had continued to make motorcycles after the war, the latest Brough Superior might look very much like a Hesketh.

When the Hesketh was conceived, in the mid-to-late 1970s, the market for superbikes was booming. With the possible exception of BMW, what was conspicuously lacking was a big, powerful, beautifully finished motorcycle built to appeal to those who, if they drove cars instead of riding bikes, would buy a Rolls Royce or a Bristol: in short, a gentleman's motorcycle.

The idea of the Hesketh was not just raw speed, though it was intended from the very beginning that there should be plenty of that. Rather, it was to be an all-round motorcycle, one which would hold its own with the majority of sports bikes but which would, at the same time, allow the rider to cover large distances in comfort at high speeds. For appraisal, Lord Hesketh bought three motorcycles, with three different engine layouts and three different reputations: a Ducati, a BMW and a three-cylinder Yamaha. With help of the same design team that had made his name famous in Formula One car racing, he worked out the parameters for the new motorcycle. The final decision was for a large-capacity V-twin. The capacity was originally to have been 900cc, but in the end the full litre won out; having a certain magic which the smaller capacity could not equal. After all, the other two great British dream bikes, the Brough Superior and the Vincent, are both remembered best for their 1000cc bikes.

Hesketh's 'Flying Chicken'.

The lineage of the engine was, broadly, by Weslake out of Cosworth. Weslake had plenty of experience in building big V-twin speedway engines, and it was Cosworth engines which powered the Hesketh Formula One cars. The wildly oversquare dimensions of the motorcycle engine (70 × 95 mm) are certainly similar to those of the racing cars; and the four-valve heads, each with its own belt-driven twin overhead cams, also owe a great deal to automobile racing practice. The choice of four cams was admittedly influenced by fashion, but a four-valve head with push-rods would probably have been harder and more expensive to make, and four-valve heads were essential for the sort of effortless performance which was envisaged, especially in the mid-range.

The crankshaft was a casting, rather than being built up, which inevitably meant split-bearing con-rods. Primary drive to the five-speed box was by gears. A four-speed box would have been more than adequate – given the

torque spread of the engine – but five speeds were once again dictated by *The Hesketh V1000.* fashion, and made the shifts slightly smoother for the fumble-footed. And even then one tester marvelled in a magazine report at the fact that the bike 'only needed' five gears! One wonders what he was used to riding. Chain final drive was chosen in place of a shaft, in the interests of lower weight and greater efficiency (on a conventionally mounted V-twin, using shaft drive means that the drive must be taken through *two* right angles, with attendant power losses). The chain was, however, laid out properly, so that the final drive sprocket was co-axial with the swinging-arm pivot: this removed all the usual problems of variation in chain tension with suspension travel, and allowed very reasonable chain life. The addition of a fully-enclosed oil-bath chain case, which is quite feasible and is one of the improvements being contemplated at the time of writing, would reduce chain maintenance to almost nothing, prolong chain life indefinitely, and still weigh less, cost less and provide greater efficiency than a shaft drive.

The full parallelogram rear brake linkage gives riders a taste of racing

braking, and indeed the brakes (by Brembo) are one of the most outstanding features of the machine. Mick Broom, the Chief Engineer, put his racing experience to work here, as elsewhere. The frame is of Reynolds 531, and can be supplied either powder coated or nickel plated (not chrome, because chromium plating embrittles the tubing). The plating on the frame, and the paintwork on the tank and elsewhere are of a quality which is hard to believe, and hard to obtain, too, because hardly anyone is still prepared to work to these standards.

The design parameters of the 1000cc (actually 992cc) motor envisaged a theoretical maximum power delivery at the crankshaft of around 120 bhp. The intention was to build a standard engine which delivered 80 plus bhp, with perhaps a 95 bhp super-sports version, and 110–115 bhp available for racing, where longevity would not be important. The actual power output on the production bikes is just under the 80 bhp mark in most cases, but some idea of the longevity of the engine may be gained from the fact that even at 30,000 and 40,000 miles, the original honing marks in the huge cylinders are still visible, and the engine is not considered fully run in until the bike has covered four or five thousand miles. There is enough metal in the cylinder walls for about ten rebores, so the life of the engine would normally be measured in *millions* of miles. The same over-engineering is

apparent in the gearbox: those huge wheels simply do not wear, at least detectably. The size of the wheels does, however, account for the well-publicised complaints about the gearbox, which is distinctly crunchy by modern Japanese standards. On the other hand, anyone used to traditional British motorcycles, or even to a BMW, will wonder what all the fuss is about. Certainly, you crunch it at first; but even a short ride, (ten or twenty miles) sees you changing gear absolutely noiselessly, except when you think about it. I must confess that I can still crunch the gears on my R100RS if I stop to think about what I am doing, but normally there is not the slightest untoward noise.

Actually, the gearbox (and some other parts such as the cam drive) are under serious consideration for lightening. The massive over-engineering was simply because no-one at Hesketh really knew how lightly certain components could be built, because most modern motorcycles are built at the limits of their materials' strength, rather than for the utmost longevity. It should be possible to lighten various components quite considerably without having any effect at all on quality or lasting ability, but resulting in a lighter, faster-responding and slightly cheaper motorcycle with improved fuel economy, good news all round!

On the subject of fuel economy, the Hesketh is fitted with 36 mm Dell'Ortos, which provide an admirably clean exhaust at normal engine speeds and reward the gentle rider with 50 mpg or more (62.5 mpg at a constant 70 mph). Most riders will see something in the 40–50 mpg range, but hard acceleration (or even blipping the throttle when the bike is at a standstill) brings the accelerator pumps into play, and fuel consumption takes a nose dive. What Mick Broom calls 'normal hard riding', which in his case might be taken to mean race-proven riding at speeds which astonish even the Germans, can bring the fuel consumption down into the mid-30s. One journalist, who presumably liked the noise that he got when he tweaked the loud tap at traffic lights, managed to break the 30 mpg barrier. Even so, there is a $5\frac{1}{2}$ gallon tank, enough for well over 200 miles of fast touring, or about 150 miles of sheer lunacy.

It may seem that I am falling into the usual trap of the nostalgia brigade, and ignoring the faults of a motorcycle whose faults have been widely criticised and are well known; but I do not believe this is so. The gearbox really is not a problem, and as for the assertion that you need to be at least six feet tall to ride a Hesketh, the seat padding is supplied to the customer's requirements. I am five foot, ten inches tall and had no problems: Mick Broom is a good two inches shorter than I, and rides a Hesketh regularly, and a little experiment showed that it was (just!) possible to adjust the seat height so that my wife (at five foot, one inch) could ride it, while still retaining some seat padding. The only real complaints concern the howl of the primary drive – which is particularly obtrusive on the faired Vampire – and the odd noise you can sometimes provoke if you ride very slowly in first gear; some sort of chatter from the gearbox which, although it apparently causes no damage whatsoever, can be a somewhat alarming experience. For my

money, this is *the* classic V-twin of the present day, just as the Brough and Vincent were in their day.

Where this eminently desirable motorcycle originally fell down was in the commercial acumen and experience of its makers. Like all the major motorcycle manufacturers, including Honda, Yamaha, Kawasaki and so forth, they mis-read the market for high-priced superbikes, and unlike the big boys they could not afford to get their fingers burnt, or even to sell their flagship bikes as loss leaders in order to reflect glamour on the rest: after all, they only had a flagship! They also grossly underestimated the length of time that it would take to get the machine into series production, and therefore the initial capital that would be required. They were used to racing schedules, where hours and days are the usual units of reckoning, where a week is a long time and a month is half way to forever. As a result, when the bike was launched in 1980, it was not completely ready.

Caught out by both the falling market and their own mistakes, they bombed. The original press tests slated the gearbox, even though it was not really all that bad, using it as a peg on which to hang all their other objections. A great deal of time and money went into trying to rectify the mistakes, but it was simply impossible. The money ran out and the original company folded in the early summer of 1982. Many people lost a lot of money, with Lord Hesketh one of the worst hit. In addition to his financial loss, he also had to endure a lot of completely inaccurate gibes, as well as some fair criticism. It would have been understandable if he had wanted nothing more to do with the machines, but out of loyalty to those customers who had already bought bikes he retained a small core of the original design team to service the machines and to try to pick up the pieces.

At first, this was all that they meant to do, but there were still many people who wanted to buy a Hesketh – even if the company had folded – and so about six months after the original operation had failed, Hesleydon Limited began to make Heskeths again. They had been over the original design very thoroughly, and devised a package of detail changes which would both improve the bike and make it easier and cheaper to produce. They bought back parts from those who had bought them at the liquidation auction, and went back to their original suppliers for other components: and they built the bikes in the old stable block at Lord Hesketh's Eatson Neston estate, in what had been the old research-and-development section of the motorcycle company. In mid-1983, they even announced a new model, the faired Vampire, one of the few motorcycles to have had its fairing properly designed with the aid of wind-tunnel testing. And then, in June 1984, they announced the 'economy model' V1000R, which was simplified in some respects (the rear braking linkage, for example) and omitted some features such as the centre stand and the self-cancelling action of indicators.

At the time of writing, Hesketh's motorcycle builders are definitely keeping their heads down, and waiting to weather the recession. They have plans to build less than one motorcycle a week for the whole of 1985. But they are also looking towards the future, and 1986, when production might climb to five or ten motorcycles a week . . .

12
V for Japan

It would not be unduly harsh to say that the Japanese have yet to produce a classic V-twin. There were apparently some little-known pre-World War Two models, dating from the days when the Japanese had a well-deserved reputation for copying foreign machines, and the same accusation could be levelled at the Rikuo 996cc and 1186cc twins of the 1950s, which bore more than a slight resemblance to the products of Juneau Avenue. In fact, it is only in the last few years that the Japanese have seriously embraced the V-twin, and they have done so in a wide variety of ways, with an even wider variety of motives. With the endless stream of new models coming from Japan every year, generalisations may be dangerous, but there are arguably three separate streams of Japanese V-twin development. The first is the liquid-cooled transverse Honda CX series; the second is the ever-increasing number of Harley-Davidson lookalikes; and the third is the increasingly frantic efforts of the Honda marketing department to produce something new.

Of the three, the Honda CX probably comes closest to achieving classic status, if only on the grounds of commercial success. Introduced in 1979, it enjoyed an unusually long production run for a large Japanese motorcycle, albeit with an increase in capacity (to 650cc) for the 1983 season. Often attacked as rather dull and suffering, at first, from a well-deserved reputation for devouring cam chains, it is technically fascinating: an 80° liquid-cooled transverse twin, with push-rod valve operation in place of the usual Honda overhead cams, and the cylinders rotated from what might seem their logical position in order to keep the carburettors out of the way of the rider's knees. Once you have accepted the 80° included angle, which makes for a (slightly) slimmer motorcycle and an improved riding position, the rest falls into place. The twisted-round cylinders are no more than a continuation of the same philosophy, and push-rod valve operation is far more sensible than the tortuous cam-drive arrangements (and increased engine height) which would be needed for overhead cams. In one sense, the CX series is no more than another variation on the BMW/Moto Guzzi theme explored in Chapter 8; in another, it represents a radical re-think of the best way of using the transverse-V layout.

The original CX500 developed 45 bhp, but evolution took it first to 50 bhp as the CX 500C, and then to 64 bhp in 650cc (actually 670cc) guise. Perhaps better than any other motorcycle in this book, the CX series illustrates the simple truth that the superbikes of yesteryear were, by modern standards, unbelievably low-powered. The Vincent Rapide only ever had 45 bhp, and the Shadow 55 bhp, from a 1000cc motor. It also illustrates how heavy

Heavy metal for dirt enthusiasts – the mighty Honda XLV.

modern motorcycles have become: the CX650E Euro Sport is within a few pounds of the weight of the Series C Rapide, and the CX 500 is only a few pounds lighter, but the Rapide's top speed of 125 mph (or better) still compares favourably with the CX 650. Most riders also report considerably better fuel consumption from the older bike, though the way in which they ride may account for a great deal of this.

There have been a number of variants on the CX theme, including a 400cc version for some European countries where there are tax or licence advantages in the smaller capacity (in some countries there are graded driving tests for different engine sizes), a turbocharged 100 bhp version of the CX 650, and the Silver Wing tourer. The 400cc version was generally agreed to be underpowered, the turbo version to be overpowered and the Wing to be overweight, but they do illustrate a commendable desire on Honda's part to get the most out of an unusually versatile motorcycle. The choice of the CX for turbocharging was all but incomprehensible, and even Honda gave as one of their reasons the argument that if they could turbocharge that, they could turbocharge anything! But everyone who has ridden the machine agrees that it far exceeds their expectations. As an early turbo, and the only turbocharged model of a popular line, the CX 650T must

surely be one of the great collectors' bikes of the future, though we shall return to the 'classic' status of Japanese bikes at the end of this chapter.

*Honda CX650T Turbo –
probably* **the** *classic in the
generally uninspiring CX
series.*

By contrast with the CX 650 T, the Silver Wing was definitely an also-ran. The original CX 500 was a first-class basic touring bike, but adding a huge fairing and bringing the weight up to nearly 490 lb did nothing to improve the performance or the handling, and using the title Silver Wing clearly showed that it was the poor man's Gold Wing. It may enjoy a certain cult status in years to come, but it can hardly be called a classic.

The various Yamahas are as different from the Hondas as chalk from cheese. The CX series could never be accused of being good-looking motorcycles, but they did bear evidence of original engineering thought. The Yamahas, on the other hand, were all about appearance and the engineering had to be fitted in around that. The original models were the 750cc and 1000cc air-cooled 75° twins, with the usual Japanese gear-driven balance shafts to help damp out the vibration. The reasoning behind the unusual angle is clear enough, though, in that it is wide enough to allow decent cooling and a respectable power output (an alleged 70 bhp in the case of the 1000cc machine), but still narrow enough to look like a Harley-Davidson. There was never much doubt at the market at which it was aimed, and one reviewer was moved to comment that Yamaha had started with a clean sheet of paper, carbon paper!

Yamaha TR1 – Japan's first water-cooled Harley lookalike.

Interestingly, the original European 750s were offered with shaft drive, presumably because Yamaha saw them as appealing to the touring market, but the 1000cc TR1 had a chain because it was a sports motorcycle. Neither of these air-cooled models was a success in the European market. Introduced for the 1981 model year in the UK, they had been discontinued by 1984. In the United States, however, the story was different. They did manage to hit the market they were aiming at, despite discriminatory legislation intended to help Harley-Davidson, and went from strength to strength. Under the Virago name, and always with shaft drive, there appeared first a 750, then a 920, and (at the time of writing) a 981cc version, with lashings of chrome and surprisingly good handling. This formula – a liquid-cooled narrow-angle engine with shaft drive, in a traditionally styled twin-rear-shock frame and a fat rear tyre – was to be adopted by all subsequent Harley rip-offs, despite the fact that Harleys were air-cooled and pioneered the return of belt transmission.

There was another Yamaha V-Twin, the XZ550 with water-cooled 70° motor, but it was remarkably unsuccessful. Introduced in the UK in 1981 for the 1982 model year, it lasted less than two years. No one is quite sure why it died, as it was apparently a sweet-handling middleweight with nearly 65 bhp and shaft drive, but nobody loved it. After the success of the Virago in America, all three of the other major Japanese manufacturers weighed in

139

with their own offerings, though at the time of writing they were all available for the American market only. The first was the original Honda 700 Shadow, with a 45° motor apparently related to the VT500E (see below) despite the difference in angle; like the VT500E, it used staggered crankpins and liquid cooling. Styling was American-Honda, heavy and chrome-ridden, but because it was quieter, faster, lighter, more reliable (at least in the short term) and above all cheaper than the Harley, it succeeded; and following the motto that 'nothing succeeds like excess', the 1985 season saw a titanic 1100cc version tricked out with high, droopy handlebars and a split-level seat with backrest. Like any motorcycle equipped with such bars, it is impossible to ride for any distance at any sort of speed, but for short or slow rides, it looked very convincing.

Kawasaki were next to fall, with the Vulcan. This was powered by a 700cc 55° liquid-cooled motor and was rather more convincingly styled; the mock-fins on the barrels (obligatory in Harley imitations) looked slightly better, and the line of the tank and stepped seat were also more Harley-like. The seat was great to look at, if you like that sort of thing, but ergonomically not quite so wonderful. The motor boasted four valves and two plugs per cylinder together with Harley-style hydraulic valve lifters. At the time of writing, it was too early to draw any conclusions, but given Kawasaki's

Intricate die-castings (from VT250 camboxes) show why restoring Japanese classics may not be easy when spares run out.

Packing in the technology – the VT250F engine.

reputation for very strong engines, and for development rather than the relentless pursuit of novelty, it might be that this is one of the V-twins of the future.

Suzuki manufactured the last imitation Harley to appear at the time of writing, in accordance with their reputation for letting Honda do the market research first. Their shaft-drive Intruder, which appeared in Canada just as I was putting the final touches to the manuscript was powered by – surprise, surprise – a 45° liquid-cooled V-twin. The styling, though, was much less extreme than either the Vulcan or the Shadow: the seat was stepped, it is true, but a least it had handlebars which were much more workmanlike than either the Honda or the Kawasaki. On the other hand, the poseur value of the machine was probably not as high as that of the others, which probably counts for a lot in that market ...

The third design stream, the thrashings around of the Honda design department, is much harder to assess. There have been some intriguing motorcycles, and if they had come from anyone other than Honda they might have been hailed as exciting new departures, or the work of an enthusiast. As it is, Honda cries wolf with so many new models every season that it is hard to summon up any enthusiasm when they bring out something that really is new, and it is very hard to distinguish the gimmickry from the innovation.

The VT250, one of the smallest in-line V-twins ever made, certainly looks like innovation. A conventionally mounted liquid-cooled 90° motor, with four valves and two overhead cams per head, finished in dramatic black, and mounted in a compact red-finished frame with 16-inch front/18-inch rear wheels, it looks very impressive; and with 35 bhp to propel it, the performance is startling. At the time of writing, it is impossible to tell whether it will last, or whether something else will replace it; but with its jewel-like construction and looks, excellent performance and apparently very fair handling, it deserves to be some sort of classic.

Honda's VT250 – state of the art engineering in a dinky V-twin.

The VT500E is a rather different sort of machine, in that it is (according to Honda) the forerunner of the series which will replace the CX. It certainly looks more like a motorcycle than a CX, but although its engine looks more conventional, it is scarcely less radical. The 52° included angle may hark back to the days of the traditional V-twin, but this is the machine which introduced the staggered crank-pin bottom end, allowing better balance and a more even firing interval than any conventional V-twin of the same included angle. It is worth remembering that this is not entirely new – the experimental Brough engine used a two-throw crankshaft – but it is certainly a major innovation in a production motorcycle, and may yet prove to be the wave of the future.

The VT500E has been produced in other capacities – both larger and smaller – for different markets, but in most cases it has been liquid-cooled, which is almost inevitable for a relatively narrow-angle V-twin with a respectable power output. There has, however, been one 'air-cooled' derivative, a titanic 750cc trail bike aimed principally at the French market, where Paris-Dakar replicas and the like were *the* poseurs' machines of the early-to-mid 1980s. The reason for placing air cooled in quotation marks is that the motor is effectively oil-cooled, with a massive increase in sump capacity and the oil circulating through the frame, in a desperate attempt to get rid of some of the heat. Even so, the power output of the engine has had to be decreased significantly by comparison with the liquid-cooled versions, in order to avoid excessive heat build-up in the heads. As a motorcycle, the machine has been unfavourably likened to heavy earth-moving machinery ('as much power as a JCB-3 but less manoeuvrable'), but it is technically very interesting in that it shows dramatically the limitations of air cooling when applied to narrow-angle twins.

What, then, is the future of 'classic' Japanese V-twins? There are, it seems, two objections which may well prove insurmountable: their high-tech design, and the short model life which is so typical of Japanese motorcycles. Most European classics have been relatively simple machines for which spares continue to be available for many years, and even when the

Kawasaki's Vulcan – out-grossing Harley.

supply of spares dries up, a dedicated enthusiast should be able to make up parts if he has access to the usual range of machine tools and (in extreme cases) a foundry for sand-casting from a part borrowed as a pattern. There may also be enough motorcycles surviving, and enough enthusiasts, to ensure that small-scale batch manufacturing of parts is feasible.

Japanese bikes, on the other hand, use sophisticated designs with highly-stressed parts and (usually) intricate die-castings. Reproducing these parts on a small scale would be prohibitively expensive, or even impossible. They also have some very dubious design features, such as running hardened steel cams directly in light-alloy heads: wonderful as long as lubrication is perfect, but disastrous if an oilway is blocked or if the machine is neglected. The life of these machines may, therefore, be inherently more limited than that of the old masters.

This is not to say that there will not be enthusiasts, or that the inherently reliable design of many Japanese machines cannot be made to run for many years to come; but there must be the suspicion that it will never be possible to rescue a Japanese motorcycle from a rusty and neglected heap at the back of someone's garage, or from a basket case of pieces disassembled many years before and never reassembled, at least not in the same way that so many classics have been preserved in the past. I hope that I am wrong.

13
Now and Hereafter

Throughout the history of motorcycling, the position of the V-twin has been uncertain. In the earliest days its main attraction was that it provided a means of getting the maximum possible swept volume from a relatively simple and compact engine, which fitted neatly into a motorcycle frame, and which was both easier to start and more tractable than a big single. There were also a few who saw the small V-twin as an elegant, smooth, high-revving engine but they were (and have always remained) in the minority.

As motorcycle design progressed and bhp/litre outputs rose steadily, it became quite possible to get more than adequate performance out of the smaller, lighter, simpler and cheaper single: two names which will forever be associated with high-performance singles are Norton and Velocette, though true *afficionados* of singles would add Rudge to that list. The development of the V-twin therefore split in two. One stream concentrated on torque, and the reliability of a big, understressed engine. The other stream was the 'super-sports' bike, where the simple aim was to produce the ultimate (or something close to it) in speed and acceleration.

The 'stump-pullers' were typified by the old side-valve Matchlesses of the 1920s and 1930s, though there were many other bikes with similar specifications and performance. Hitched to sidecars of sometimes astonishing size and weight, they provided family transport for the man who could not afford a motor-car, or who (more rarely) was so enamoured of motorcycles that he actually preferred his 'outfit' to a car. Many tradesmen used side-cars as well: the window-cleaner, with his box sidecar carrying ladders, buckets and cloth, remained a common sight into the 1950s, though by that time precious few of them were still using V-twins. The other major users of the under-stressed V-twin were the police of many countries, who appreciated the reliability that the design brought and found the motorcycle both cheaper and more convenient than the motor-car for getting policemen to where they were needed. It is also important to remember that the performance of the ordinary motor-car has improved immensely since about 1950, and particularly since 1960. In the pre-war years even the less sporting V-twin motorcycles were more than a match for almost anything on four wheels.

This line of development was, however, slowly crushed by the development of the cheap motor-car, which offered full weather protection, greater comfort and easier handling in the hands of a novice. The police still hung on to their motorcycles, but the gradual disappearance of the sidecar market which made production economical and the increasing adoption of 'patrol

cars' in a less economy-conscious age meant that their choice became ever more limited. By the 1980s, the BMW was almost the automatic choice of police-forces the world over, though paradoxically the big flat twins died even as they were still conquering new markets: the San Francisco Police Department bought BMWs in 1984, in the year when the 1000cc 'boxers' were on their way out. The superbike market, on the other hand, was always precarious. The earliest V-twin superbikes were made by Indian, Harley-Davidson and Matchless in the second decade of the twentieth century, but by the 1920s the American firms had lost their technical lead for ever and Matchless, like most others, concentrated on side-car stump-pullers. There were still a few ultra-high-performance machines, such as the Crocker in America, but it was the Brough Superior which captured the public imagination. In the depressed 1930s, the single became *the* sporting machine for most people, and the big-capacity V-twins tended to stagnate technically – though such machines as the Vincent-HRD were still fairly advanced superbikes by any standards.

After World War Two, there were very few firms left making V-twins for any purpose. Apart from very limited-production (and limited-interest) machines such as the little Japanese Lilac and the German Victoria, there was the massive and incredibly old-fashioned Harley-Davidson and the superb Vincent, the fastest production motorcycle in the world. But Vincent was always in financial trouble, and with their disappearance in the mid-

1950s it might have seemed quite reasonable to write off the V-twin as an evolutionary dead-end in the history of motorcycle design. In fact, the Milwaukee company survived because of a large and traditionally-minded home market, aided in later years by wholly un-American protectionist trade barriers. By the mid-1980s Harley-Davidson were definitely hanging on by the skin of their teeth.

But yet ... but yet ... the Japanese marketing revolution, which had shown the world that you did not have to be an unwashed man-mountain with grease permanently under your fingernails in order to ride a motorcycle (something that BMW riders had known since 1923), also created a market for bigger bikes, with outstanding performance, but built to the same oil-tight and reliable standards as the lightweights with which the Japanese had made their name. The term 'superbike' was about to be coined.

The market for big bikes had long been dominated by the parallel twin, except in the United States where Harley-Davidson still ruled the roost. But the parallel twin which is wonderful at 500cc, is good at 650cc, barely tolerable at 750cc and a disaster at anything bigger. Japanese high-tech parallel twins of 350cc and 450cc capacity already developed more power than many 750cc bikes from the old school, and the Japanese knew that bigger parallel twins would bring more problems than they solved.

The result was a glut of transverse four-cylinder engines, a layout which had been tried for racing in the 1930s but (rightly) dismissed as too big, too

wide, too heavy, too expensive and with too high a centre of gravity for road use. Despite their obvious drawbacks, people bought these things! The reason, of course, was that the biggest market was America, where cornering was not so much a lost art, as one which had never existed. Determined bend-swingers, in the Californian canyons for example, still bought British or Italian bikes, and learned to live with oil leaks on the former, appalling finish on the latter, and disgraceful electrics on both.

This worked well enough in the 1960s and (very) early 1970s, but people began to clamour for machines which combined the power, covenience, reliability and finish of the Japanese machines with the handling of European motorcycles. The first generation of superbikes had provided the raw power; the second generation was faced with the question of how to tame it.

Several European manufacturers, spying a bandwagon, jumped on to it. The Ducati twins were perhaps the classic solution, but they were still too much in the Italian sports mould for many tastes: rock-hard suspension and board-like saddles, kick-start only, and (still) indifferent electrics, instrumentation and finish. The Moto-Guzzi transverse twins were rather more original, and more suitable for the general rider in every way, but the engine showed its antecedents. It was not even a motorcycle engine to begin with, and there was very little more power to be extracted from it without going to four-valve heads. Several Japanese manufacturers saw salvation in the V-

148

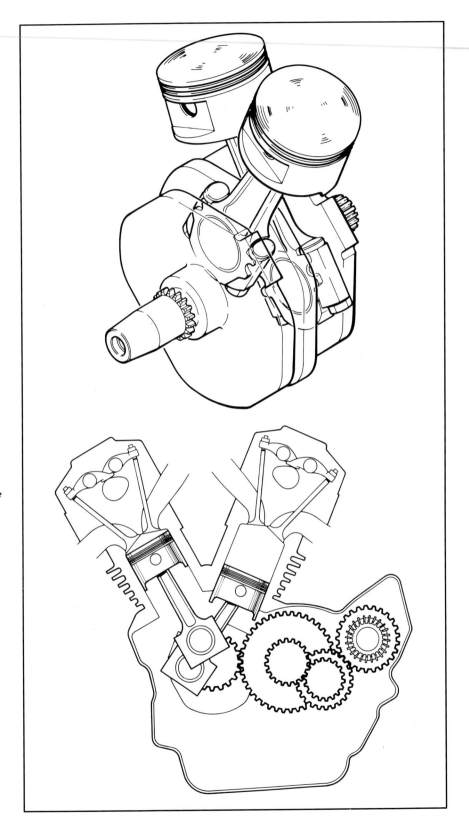

Staggered crankpins balance the firing interval on Honda VT twins – but balance shafts still echo the 'Universal Japanese Motorcycle'.

twin and, as mentioned, Lord Alexander Fermor Hesketh saw it as the configuration with which to enter the top end of the motorcycle market.

But two things conspired against this last generation of V-twins. The first, was an unforeseen world recession, which seriously depressed the superbike market. After all, superbikes are scarcely essential for anyone's lifestyle, and are generally bought out of disposable income when other priorities have already been taken care of. The second, was an increasingly hard line from the governments of the world in anti-motorcycle legislation.

To be fair, not all of it was intended to be specifically anti-motorcycle; but in many cases, ignorance and lack of thought on the part of the legislators meant that this was the effect. For example, anti-pollution laws are generally agreed to be desirable, but politicians who had never ridden motorcycles never stopped to think about the weight and expense that a catalytic exhaust-gas cleaner would add to a motorcycle. Still less did they think about the fact that such converters would run very hot indeed and would be a major risk on a normally-running motorcycle, quite apart from being an almost certain fire-starter in a spill. Again, the noise regulations enacted in many countries discriminate in a ridiculous manner against precisely those bikes which most people would regard as the quietest. Because the tests specify the engine speed at which the moving noise tests must be conducted, (relatively) slow-revving four-strokes such as the BMW and the Hesketh are turning over rather faster than they would normally be run, whilst two-stroke screamers are running unnaturally slowly and quietly. Consequently, the valve clatter of a BMW (which few people even notice) is accorded disproportionate importance, whilst the howl of an overworked two-stroke (a noise which even motorcyclists dislike after they have outgrown adolescence) is minimised. It might seem that these objections, legitimate as they are, might carry some weight, but unfortunately three things conspire against their doing so.

The first is that most politicians are completely ignorant of all technical matters, and would not understand technical arguments even if they were presented with them. This is an almost inevitable, but sickening, corollary of democracy.

The second is that changing the law would be admitting that they had made a mistake. As is well known, politicians never make mistakes, so the existing legislation must be right in the first place.

The third is that there is a genuine bias against motorcycling and motorcyclists. There are several reasons for this, but the root cause is that a motorcycle is a symbol of freedom, and if there is one thing that no politician can stand it is freedom. Even those who speak in its favour do not use the word in its conventional meaning, namely 'in charge of one's own destiny, free of restrictions', but rather 'in accordance with my view of freedom, without the restrictions which my opponent would impose'. As a result, politicians of all schools combine to place restrictions upon the motorcyclist. For example, in the United Kingdom, right-hand sidecars were banned because it was 'obvious' that they were dangerous. No statistics

One bike no-one would mind riding at dusk on a wet road – a Super Darmah 900 Desmo.

150

The murderous complexity of Honda's V-fours is a strong argument for V-twins.

Left and opposite: Moto-Guzzi show clearly how the same basic machine can be made to appeal to different markets, with these three models from their 1984 range.

whatsoever were produced to support this argument, 'everybody knew that it was true,' despite the fact that not a single accident was found that could be traced to a right-hand chair! In Japan, it is illegal to sell any motorcycle over 750cc, except imported models. This leads to the ridiculous situation of Japanese-made bikes being exported and then re-imported in order to get around the law. In Germany, there is a 'gentleman's agreement' not to build or import motorcycles of over 100 bhp, an agreement which would become law if anyone seriously tried to transgress it. Russia will admit motorists from the decadent west, but not motorcyclists, and in at least one Scandinavian country there has been serious talk of banning *all* motorcycles. The Nanny State, who knows what is best for everyone, says that motorcycles are nasty dangerous things and good little children don't play with them; no wonder alcohol and suicide are so popular in Scandinavia! Faced with this sort of attitude, the motorcyclist can hardly be surprised when his legitimate technical complaints are ignored, or even when they lead to already foolish laws being adminstered all the more harshly when it becomes clear that the loser will be the motorcyclist. In one American state, a rider was even successfully prosecuted when he took one hand off the bars to make a signal. The policeman thought, and the judge agreed, that this meant he was unable to control the machine properly.

A side-effect of all this has been that it has become absurdly expensive for manufacturers to meet all the regulations that have been forced upon them. In Britain in 1984, for instance, an official noise test cost £2,000 – an almost impossible burden for a small firm – and the full fee was payable for each test, which automatically became legally compulsory when anything was done which could affect the noise output of the motorcycle.

Ignoring the possibility of an out-and-out ban, the main problems facing motorcycle manufacturers are three-fold. The first is noise control; the second is emission control (air pollution control); and the third is marketing. The question of limitations on power outputs is mainly academic, unless quite drastic reductions are called for, because emission control and noise control between them will quite effectively take the edge off performance. Where does this leave the V-twin?

Paradoxically, it takes us back to where we began this chapter. Keeping an engine quiet and cleaning up its exhaust means a significant reduction in power, or a significant increase in weight, or both. The V-twin is simple enough to be built reasonably lightly, allows plenty of swept volume, and fits as well into a motorcycle frame as it ever did. In other words, it sends us straight back to the early days of motorcycle design. Of course, the V-twin is only one possible solution. BMW's in-line water-cooled four, laid on its side, is as elegant a solution to the problems of the present day as the flat-twin was to the demands of the twenties (and thirties, and forties and fifties . . .). But the BMW layout is so revolutionary (even if it has been tried before as an Ariel prototype) that for anyone else to produce it would lead to accusations of plagiarism, a bad thing from a marketing point of view. The transverse water-cooled four is a possibility, but almost certainly too heavy and ungainly (though that was said about air-cooled fours, too). The water-cooled flat four, Honda Goldwing-style, is an excellent design (and one that BMW must have considered), but it is *very* wide and heavy. Not even the most dedicated Wing rider defends his machine as a sports bike. The water-cooled V-four is impossibly complicated and hard to work on, and there are signs of a reaction against this trend in motorcycle design, so it can probably be discounted (though I would not lay money on it). Sixes have never been particularly popular, except for the extremes of racing and of posing. This

The basic Honda V-twin of the late 80s, the VT500E.

leaves the single, which cannot develop enough power for a modern superbike; the parallel twin, which despite balance shafts still vibrates horribly at anything much over 500cc; the in-line triple, which may have some possibilities but shares several of the disadvantages of both the parallel twin and the in-line four, unless made with a 120° crankshaft; and the V-twin. The triple must remain a contender, but the future of the V-twin for high-performance motorcycling looks at least as good as it has ever done.

Of course, the engine will be made as efficient as possible. High thermal efficiency (extracting the maximum possible amount of work from the fuel burned) is not only good news for fuel economy, but also results in cleaner exhaust as well. The four-valve head will probably continue to be the standard design, with conventional overhead-cam valve actuation: this is not only efficient, but quieter than push-rods as well. Cam drive will probably be by toothed belt, in the interests of cost and quiet running. Desmodromic heads are probably an evolutionary dead-end: two-valve desmo designs are no more efficient than four-valve valve-spring designs, and four-valve desmo heads would be alarmingly expensive and complicated to make. In the more distant future, ceramic engine components are likely: these can run at very

155

much higher temperatures (and hence very much more efficiently) than metal parts.

The ultra-rare Wallis 1928 – the steering of the future?

Contrary to popular belief, water cooling is not absolutely essential for noise reduction (though it is very useful), but it is invaluable for cooling highly-efficient cylinder heads. Water cooling, or perhaps oil cooling (because oil can run at very much higher temperatures than even a pressurised water system) is therefore extremely likely in V-twins of the future and, indeed, on any other configuration. The only danger with oil cooling is that it could run very hot indeed, with terrible results in the case of a smash or even a split radiator.

One of the major problems in noise control, though, could make a nonsense of all that I have said so far. Believe it or not, induction roar is one of the biggest sources of noise in a motorcycle engine, and it may be that the future lies either in *very* small engines of unbelievably high thermal efficiency, or in large, slow-running engines with very restricted breathing, in which case, push-rods and water-cooling will be more than enough and there will be no cause for ceramic components unless their price drops far enough to make them economically attractive. In fact, a prototype for such an engine (without ceramics) already exists, in the form of the Honda CX series of transverse twins. Often decried as 'gutless', and scorned as the 'plastic maggot', the CX500 may well point the way towards a whole school of motorcycle design. It is true that it is scarcely a super-sports machine, but the performance is perfectly respectable for a 500cc motorcycle, and if it did not eat cam chains it would be hard to fault it in its chosen role.

There are also other predictions which could be made concerning the future of the motorcycle, such as the probable increase in the use of toothed-belt final drive (quietness and reliability again), the adoption of hub-centre steering (seen by many designers as inevitable), and the radical redesign of the frame, whether in 'feet-forward' Malcolm Newell style or in a form more closely resembling the conventional motorcycle, though there is probably room for both and if one does go under it is likely to be the feet-forward style, because of the innate conservatism of so many motorcyclists. And this brings us back to marketing, as well as providing a good excuse to abandon futurology (I have stuck my neck out far enough already).

The V-twin has a classic appeal, which has persisted for over three-quarters of a century. So many superbikes have been V-twins that almost everyone includes at least one V-twin in his private list of the half dozen machines that he would most like to own. It is a tried and true layout, and one that is easy to work on. The wild profusion of engine types of the early 1980s, most of which proved unsuccessful, has encouraged at least a partial return to the values of the past. We have seen the collapse of the worst excesses of the 'new-model-every-year' syndrome in motor-cars, and badly burned fingers among all the major Japanese manufacturers may mean that the same will happen with motorcycles. So Harley-Davidson may yet prove to be in the forefront of motorcycle design, and the 'last bike from the 1950s', the Hesketh, may be one of the first bikes of the 1980s. I hope so. And even if the days of the motorcycle – any motorcycle – are numbered, well, what magnificent things they were while they lasted.

Index

Engine sizes are given as ci or cc depending on contemporary usage: where possible, cc figures are precise, for example, 645 cc rather than 650: references to illustrations are given in *italic*. Within marque, bikes are given as nearly as possible in order of development rather than in alphabetical order.